Bringing Household Services Out of the Shadows

FORMALISING NON-CARE WORK IN AND AROUND THE HOUSE

OECD

BETTER POLICIES FOR BETTER LIVES

This work is published under the responsibility of the Secretary-General of the OECD. The opinions expressed and arguments employed herein do not necessarily reflect the official views of OECD member countries.

This document, as well as any data and map included herein, are without prejudice to the status of or sovereignty over any territory, to the delimitation of international frontiers and boundaries and to the name of any territory, city or area.

The statistical data for Israel are supplied by and under the responsibility of the relevant Israeli authorities. The use of such data by the OECD is without prejudice to the status of the Golan Heights, East Jerusalem and Israeli settlements in the West Bank under the terms of international law.

Note by Turkey
The information in this document with reference to "Cyprus" relates to the southern part of the Island. There is no single authority representing both Turkish and Greek Cypriot people on the Island. Turkey recognises the Turkish Republic of Northern Cyprus (TRNC). Until a lasting and equitable solution is found within the context of the United Nations, Turkey shall preserve its position concerning the "Cyprus issue".

Note by all the European Union Member States of the OECD and the European Union
The Republic of Cyprus is recognised by all members of the United Nations with the exception of Turkey. The information in this document relates to the area under the effective control of the Government of the Republic of Cyprus.

Please cite this publication as:
OECD (2021), *Bringing Household Services Out of the Shadows: Formalising Non-Care Work in and Around the House*, OECD Publishing, Paris, *https://doi.org/10.1787/fbea8f6e-en*.

ISBN 978-92-64-73758-7 (print)
ISBN 978-92-64-91576-3 (pdf)

Foreword

With *Dare to Share: Germany's Experience Promoting Equal Partnership in Families* (OECD, 2017[1]) and *Good Practice for Good Jobs in Early Childhood Education and Care* (OECD, 2019[2]) the OECD Social Policy Division previously explored issues around parental care for children and the quality of formal childcare arrangements. This report is the first project in the OECD Social Policy Division that focuses on the area of domestic services, and policies that are geared towards the formalisation of non-care work.

Following increasing female employment rates and widespread informality, policies in the non-care household service sector have become important instruments to help families combine their careers with their housework burden. However, international approaches differ markedly in their impact on reducing the incidence of informal work arrangements and boosting employment among low-skilled and unemployed workers and this report analyses and compares the approaches in five countries with extensive policies: Belgium, Finland, France, Germany and Sweden.

This report was written by Willem Adema and Jonas Fluchtmann (OECD Social Policy Division) under the supervision of Monika Queisser (Senior Counsellor, Head of the OECD Social Policy Division). Liv Gudmundson prepared the report for publication, with Lucy Hulett, Fatima Perez and Jayne Maddock providing further logistical, publication and communications support. The OECD gratefully acknowledges the financial support by the German Federal Ministry of Family Affairs, Senior Citizens, Women and Youth towards the preparation of this study.

The analysis benefitted from inputs and insights from the participants of the OECD expert consultation on the formalisation of non-care household services. Special thanks to Clément Carbonnier (Université Paris 8), Karin Halldén (Stockholm University), Ive Marx (University of Antwerp), Holger Bonin (IZA Bonn), Jarkko Harju (Tampere University), Nuria Ramos Martín (University of Amsterdam) and Thomas Fischer (German Federal Ministry of Family Affairs, Senior Citizens, Women and Youth). We also thank Jorrit Zwijnenburg (OECD Statistics and Data Directorate) and Peter van de Ven (previously OECD Statistics and Data Directorate) for their guidance in estimating the economic value of unpaid housework. We are further grateful for comments provided by Aurélie Decker (European Federation for Services to Individuals), Julien Freund (Sodexo), Stijn Broecke (OECD Skills and Employability Division) and Monika Queisser (Senior Counsellor, Head of the OECD Social Policy Division).

4 |

Table of contents

TABLES

Follow OECD Publications on:

http://twitter.com/OECD_Pubs

http://www.facebook.com/OECDPublications

http://www.linkedin.com/groups/OECD-Publications-4645871

http://www.youtube.com/oecdilibrary

http://www.oecd.org/oecddirect/

Executive summary

In 2019, on average 1.3% of the registered labour force in OECD countries were employed as non-care household service workers, and many more engage in undeclared work in this sector. These workers, most of which are women, provide a variety of services that support households in their daily life, such as cleaning, laundry, gardening and cooking. With increased time stress within households, these services can be an important contributor to the well-being of families. This is particularly important for women, who spend more than twice as much time per day on unpaid non-care housework than do men. Despite its unpaid nature, conservative estimates suggest that non-care housework contributes as much to our economic well-being as the average value added by the manufacturing sector in the OECD.

The relatively high formal labour cost for low-income workers in many OECD countries, has contributed to the development of a large informal non-care household service sector in many countries. Undeclared workers generally lack access to social benefits, sufficient health and safety protection and/or employment-related training, which leaves many of them in vulnerable employment, social and health conditions. To reduce the incidence of informal employment, integrate vulnerable workers in the labour market, and enhance employment and career opportunities for women otherwise engaged in unpaid housework, several OECD countries have introduced a range of schemes to formalise employment and production in the non-care household service sector.

This report compares the formalisation approaches in five countries with extensive policy frameworks for non-care household services: Belgium, Finland, France, Germany and Sweden. Common to these countries are policy instruments that reduce the price of non-care household service work. Belgium and France use social vouchers, which recipients can buy at low prices or receive from their employers to pay for non-care household services. Sweden, Finland, France and Germany grant tax credits that offer different degrees of favourable tax treatment to the consumer of such services.

Social vouchers are transparent measures that are easy to use for consumers across the income distribution; they also facilitate targeting support at specific groups in the population. However, tax credits are usually claimed with the annual tax return, which requires that consumers pay the full service price upfront. This can lead to low consumption among households with lower incomes who cannot afford the higher price.

Low-income households may also not have sufficient taxable income to benefit from traditional tax credits. In response, French policy has made these tax credits refundable (i.e. they are paid out in cash to those without the necessary tax liabilities), but this has not led to substantial consumption effects at the lower end of the income distribution. The high gross service prices seem to be a substantial barrier for low-income households to overcome. However, if tax credits are granted "at source" – at the time of service consumption – as in Sweden, households with lower income find it easier to buy profit from favourable tax treatment.

Other instruments simplify the administrative processes in hiring domestic workers, for example, by outsourcing the handling of payroll and social contributions to external contractors. Particularly in countries where direct domestic employment is common, i.e. where households act as the employer of domestic workers, these systems are another important aspect of accessibility. In countries where most services are provided through intermediary provider organisations, such instruments are generally not important.

Particular design features of tax credits or social vouchers, such as limiting the use of vouchers to services bought from provider organisations, can influence the distribution of the types of work arrangements and thus the job quality in the non-care household service sector. For example, registered intermediary service providers generally offer better social and health protections than households who directly employ service workers. In addition, if direct employment is established through declarative vouchers, many households are not even aware that they have taken on employer responsibilities.

Depending on the country, both social vouchers and tax credits can be linked to a reduced incidence of informal work. However, the effectiveness depends on the extent to which service prices are reduced by tax credits/social vouchers. For example, German households can receive a tax rebate equal to 20% of their expenses on household services, while households in Sweden and France receive a rebate of 50%. The French and Swedish systems have proven to be more effective in moving informal work into the formal sector.

While support policies have generated positive employment effects among low-skilled workers and the unemployed, some systems have proven to be very attractive to labour migrants. For example, in Brussels EU labour migrants make up two-thirds of the non-care household service workforce, and initial policy objectives of the policy to integrate refugees and other vulnerable workers were difficult to achieve.

The available evidence does suggest, however, that following the introduction of non-care household service policies, higher-skilled women generally increase their labour force participation.

The public costs of non-care household services can be substantial, yet resulting reductions in the expenditure on unemployment benefits and increased public revenue can lead to considerable earn-back effects. The net costs of the formalisation policies is often estimated to be close to being budget neutral, but the underlying assumptions on job creation and unemployment reduction may well be overly optimistic. At the same time, moving informal work into the formal sector is generally associated with substantially better working conditions, (partial) coverage by labour protections and access to social benefits. While these effects cannot be measured in cost-benefit analyses, they are a critical factor for the well-being of non-care household service workers.

1 Introduction and main findings

Non-care household services are usually defined as object-centred activities that support daily living, and which are mainly carried out in the home of a customer, sometimes also referred to as indirect care.[1] However, exact definitions vary across countries as they are typically tied to specific policies and instruments in this sector. Often lumped together with care-related work under the umbrella Personal and Household Services (PHS), these activities aim to improve the well-being of households and/or support its maintenance. The main activities captured by the non-care household services label range from cleaning and ironing to maintenance and smaller repair work as well as gardening. Yet data sources and policy instruments do not always distinguish between care- and non-care types of service provision and providers may also deliver both types of services (Baga et al., 2020[3]).

There are different work arrangements in the non-care household service sector. Formal work arrangements concern either a "bipartite" relationship, i.e. direct employment by households, or "tripartite" relationships, where intermediaries, such as commercial or non-commercial service providers, employ the workers involved. In some cases the boundaries between the two are blurry, e.g. in case of platform work or micro-entrepreneurship.

However, a substantial part of household services is estimated to be provided informally. In contrast to formal employees, informal workers do not have access to social benefits, health and safety protection and/or employment-related training. The nature of the work arrangements in the sector thereby co-determines working conditions and service quality (Martin Ramos and Ruiz, 2020[4]).

High labour cost of formal workers is seen as one of the main reasons why many consumers buy household services informally. By reducing the cost of household services through tax credits or social vouchers, some OECD countries have tried to encourage the formalisation of household service provision, thereby not only moving household service workers out of the shadow economy but also freeing up time for mostly women to participate in the labour market rather than undertaking unpaid housework. In turn, this would ensure a minimum standard of working conditions in the sector, and could potentially be fiscally neutral, as increased tax revenue from increased formal labour force participation.

The analysis focuses on experiences with non-care household service policies in five countries that have had reasonably comprehensive measures in this area since the early 2000s – Belgium, Finland, France, Germany and Sweden; in addition, the report also includes headline information on measures in other OECD countries. The report first considers the size of employment in the non-care household services sector and then provides estimates on the economic value of unpaid housework in OECD households. The second part of the analysis considers the different measures in place and discusses these in terms of operational aspects such as nature of provision, services covered, value of support, ease of access, and the groups who use support. The third section gauges the effect of the policies in terms of consumption effects and groups of users, employment effects and the overall cost of the programme in view of earn-back effects.

The main findings from this report include:

- Employment in the formal non-care household services sector ranges from 0.1% to 2.9% for countries for which data are available, more than 90% of which are women. Estimates on the size of the informal workforce in this sector are not fully comparable but suggest that in some countries the informal sector covers up to 90% of all non-care household service work.

- Women spend more than twice the time per day in unpaid non-care housework than men. Policy initiatives to reduce engaging in unpaid housework and free up (more) time for labour force participation will therefore benefit women in their labour market opportunities most.

- The value of time spent on unpaid work on basis of the replacement cost approach is estimated to be around 15% of GDP, roughly equal to the average value added by the manufacturing sector in the OECD, but this increases to 27% of GDP when the opportunity costs of workers in unpaid work at home are accounted for. Women create the majority of this economic value.

- Policy measures to stimulate the formalisation of non-care household services include tax credits and (social) vouchers, which often also extend to care-related services in the household. Tax credits are considered as measures of favourable tax treatment. Social vouchers are transparent, easy to use, and can benefit all consumers across the income distribution; they also allow for simple targeting of specific groups if desired. Finland, Germany and Sweden have tax credits while the Belgian and French systems are a mix of the two, with the Belgian system being the only one with an emphasis on vouchers and covering exclusively non-care services.

- In terms of timely access to support, the Swedish tax credit system and the Belgian social voucher grant financial support to users at the moment of service use, which is an important feature for low-income users. By contrast, in France, Finland and Germany users only receive financial support towards the use of household services at the time of settling the next annual tax return, meaning that the up-front cost for consumers is substantially higher.

- To enhance the full use of service support it is important to keep administrative systems as simple as possible. Social vouchers, such as the Belgian one, which can be exchanged against service work, or the French declarative CESU system which simplifies the hiring of domestic workers, can greatly reduce the administrative burden related to household service work.

- The conditions of employment are generally more favourable in predominantly tripartite systems (services providers, employees, and households), such as in Belgium, Finland and Sweden. In these cases, intermediaries allow for better working conditions, collective bargaining and greater health and safety provisions. Direct employment relationships between the employing household and the worker are more common in France and Germany, but expose household service workers to greater risks of precarious employment.

- The policy instruments in the household service sector are used by close to 25% of households in Belgium and between 14 and 20% of households in Finland, France and Sweden. Perhaps surprisingly, the scope of services covered is not necessarily predictive of the extent to which support policies such as tax-credits or social vouchers are being used: the ability to set competitive market prices is a more important factor.

- Households of moderate- to high incomes are the main beneficiaries of the policy instruments in the household service sector. The absence of sufficient taxable income and high gross service prices are major access barriers for lower-income households. However, it is questionable whether making tax credits available to the lowest income earners can lead to sizeable consumption effects among these groups. For example, after France generalised the "refundability" of their household service tax credits, the number of household service consumers did not markedly increase. Instead, the overall volume of fiscal reimbursement for low- to moderate-income earners that already claimed tax credits increased.

- Granting tax credits "at source" makes the fee reductions more visible and reduces confusion, which can increase consumption particularly among low-income households who would find it harder to pay the full service price upfront. For example, since Sweden grants its household service tax credit at source, the number of consuming households has strongly increased.

- Social vouchers and tax credits can be linked to clear reductions in informality, particularly in countries with generous fiscal support, such as France and Sweden. However, resulting from differences in price elasticities, even relatively comparable systems, like in Finland and Sweden, can show large differences in the effectiveness of reducing informality in the household service sector. Less generous systems, like in Germany, have not seen particularly noticeable shifts to declared household service employment.

- Direct employment as prevalent in France and Germany involves households employing domestic service workers through declarative systems. However, by doing so, many households unwittingly take on employer responsibilities which could result in significant costs, especially if client households make mistakes in legal work contracts and procedures.

- In some countries, social vouchers and tax credits have led to sizeable employment in and outside of the non-care household service sector. As such, the low-skilled and unemployed workers, predominantly women, face increased employment opportunities, while higher-skilled women are able to increase their labour force participation.

- However, the long-established Belgian and Swedish systems are also very attractive to workers outside the national labour market. As such, they involve the risk that European labour migrants crowd out more vulnerable groups by entering the system. For example, foreign workers, predominantly of EU origin, make up more than two-thirds of all service voucher workers in the Belgian capital Brussels, despite high unemployment and a large labour reserve in the region. As a result, the intended objectives of integrating refugees and other low-skilled and vulnerable workers into the regular labour market cannot be achieved.

- Despite the high costs often associated with policy interventions in the non-care household service market, social vouchers and tax credits exhibit sizeable earn-back effects through reduced expenditure on unemployment benefits as well as increased public revenue. The net cost of the policy intervention is assessed to be moderate at maximum, for example in Sweden, or close to budget neutral, such as in Belgium and France, however, the underlying assumptions on net job creation may well be optimistic.

2 Non-care household services in the OECD

2.1. Formal employment

Formal sector workers are either directly employed by the households for whom they work, or they are employed by commercial or non-profit organisations who deliver household services as per contractual agreement. However, measuring employment levels in the non-care household service sector is not straightforward. Definitions of non-care household services often differ across countries and common statistical groupings for economic activities and occupations are either too broad or too narrow to adequately represent the true size of the labour force engaging in non-care household service employment.

This report follows the approach of the *PHS Industry Monitor* of the European Federation for Services to Individuals (EFSI), which is based on occupational classifications commonly used in Labour Force Surveys that, while imperfect, appears more accurate than an approach based on economic activities (EFSI, 2018[5]).[2] The approach makes use of the detailed 4-digit code International Standard Classification of Occupations (ISCO) referring to domestic cleaners and helpers (code *9111*).[3] In cases where sufficient data is not available, the broader group of domestic, hotel, and office cleaners and helpers (code *911*) can be used, while subtracting the number of non-domestic cleaners, as provided by the European Cleaning and Facility Services Industry (EFCI, 2020[6]). For some non-EU countries, national sources can be used (see the notes to Figure 2.1).

Figure 2.1 shows the share of registered non-care household service employees among all registered employment. On average, 1.3% of all registered employees in OECD countries are formally employed as non-care household service workers. There are wide differences across countries, ranging from 2.5% in Spain, Portugal and France, to as little as 0.1% of registered employees in Poland and the Czech Republic. While a break-down by sex is not available on the country level, about 93% of all registered employees in the European Union are female (see also EFSI (2018[5])).

However, the personal household service sector is regarded as one of the economic sectors where services are provided by workers that do not register all or a part of their employment activities with the responsible fiscal authorities and does not appear in official statistics (EFSI, 2018[5]; European Commission, 2018[7]). For example, the Cologne Institute for Economic Research estimates that 8.1% of all German households employ a household service provider, yet almost nine out ten are employed informally and thus do not appear in Labour Force Statistics (Enste, 2019[8]). Given this, Figure 2.1 is likely to provide only a very partial picture of the size of employment in the sector.

One of the reasons for the prevalence of undeclared work in the sector concerns the relatively high tax burden on labour cost for the low-paid workers in the sector. Customer households may deem formal services as too expensive and demand informal services to avoid paying the tax burden as reflected in the price of the service. For example, 90% of representative German households reported they use services in the informal economy because they are relatively cheap, and 68% of responding households in Germany stated they would not consume household services through the formal economy due to the high labour costs (Feld and Schneider, 2010[9]).

Figure 2.1. Registered employment in the non-care household service sector (ISCO)

Share of registered "Domestic Cleaners and Helpers" among total registered employment, 2018 or latest available year

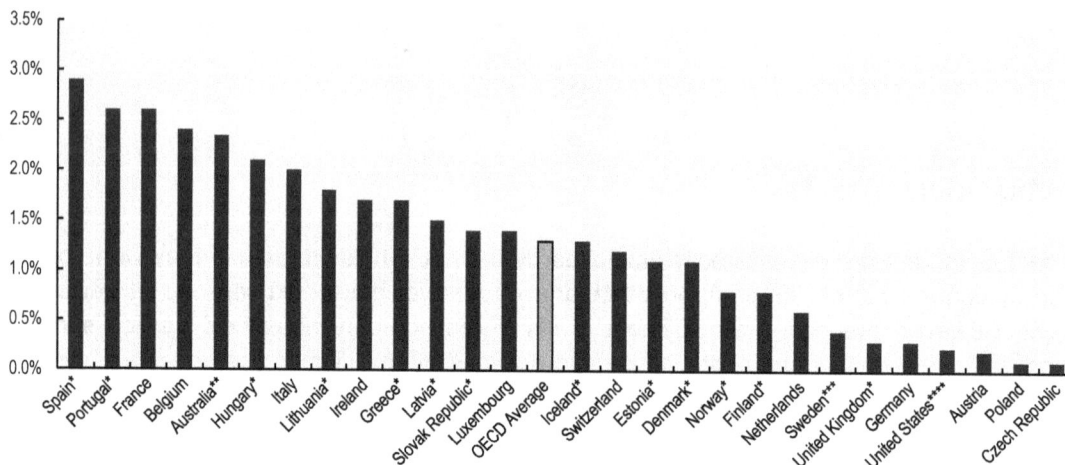

Note: Data refer to exclusively to registered workers. As unregistered employment is particularly common in PHS sector, the statistics may substantively underestimate the true extent of employment (see below). For EU countries – and where available – data refer to worker employed in category 9111 of the International Standard Classification of Occupations (ISCO) statistical nomenclature (*Domestic Cleaners and Helpers*). For non- EU countries, other related groups are presented and may slightly differ. * For these countries, no data on category 9111 was available. Instead, these numbers represent category 911 (*Domestic, Hotel, and Office Cleaners and Helpers*) subtracted by the number of cleaners in non-domestic environments, as provided by the European Cleaning and Facility Services Industry (EFCI). ** For Australia, data refer to cleaners and laundry workers (code 811) in the Australian and New Zealand Standard Classification of Occupations (ANZSCO) who are also employed by private households (code 9601) in the Australian and New Zealand Standard Industrial Classification (ANZSIC) in 2019. *** For Sweden, the data refer to registered employment in the RUT sector as reported by the Swedish Tax Authorities and thus covers care and non-care work. **** For the United States, data refer to house cleaners as per definition of the Economic Policy Institute (EPI). That is, workers who are simultaneously in the Census occupation group "maids and housekeeping cleaners" (code 4230) and the Census industry group "private household" (code 9290) in 2019.
Source: OECD calculations based on data from the European Union Labour Force Survey, the Australian Labour Force Survey, the European Cleaning and Facility Services Industry, the Economic Policy Institute, and Skatteverket.

The considerable difference between the effective net wage for low paid employees (less than 50% of countries' average earnings) and the total labour costs to the employer curtails the demand for employment. Figure 2.2 shows that the *tax wedge* – a summary measure of the overall tax burden on workers, averages about 28% for low-income workers across the OECD (OECD, 2020[10]). In Chile, Israel, Mexico and New Zealand the tax wedge is relatively low, but it exceeds 40% in Germany and Hungary, which means that low paid workers typically take home only little over a half of the price employers or consumers pay on their labour (although specific national policies can substantively reduce the tax burden on some low paid workers, see below).[4]

The labour tax burden and the associated high price for service work is not the only driver of collaborative tax evasion by consumers and service providers. Doerr and Necker (forthcoming[11]), for example, suggest that informal services are easier to access as their use avoids the administrative efforts and costs associated with employing service workers.

Figure 2.2. Tax wedge on labour costs for low paid workers

Ratio between taxes paid by single and childless workers with 50% of avg. earnings and total labour costs for employer, 2019

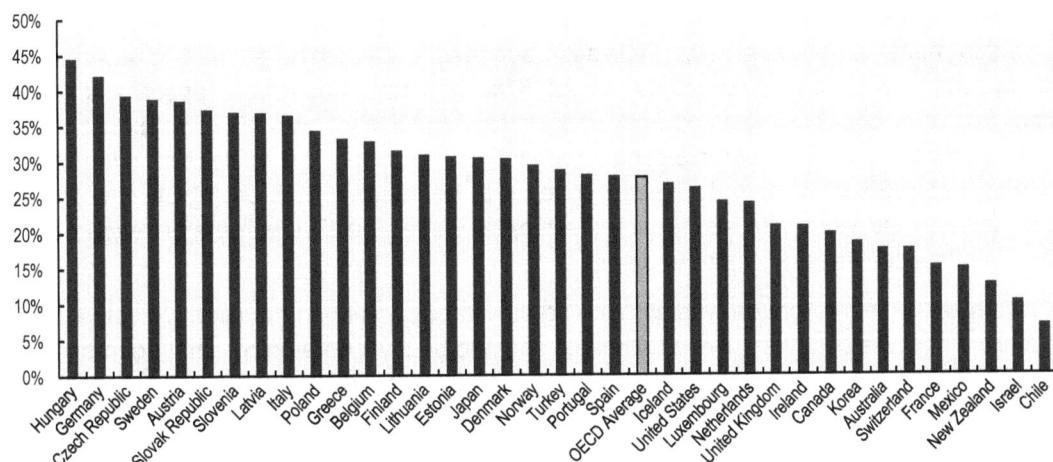

Note: Tax wedge is defined as the ratio between the amount of taxes paid by an average single without children and the corresponding total labour cost for the employer. The average tax wedge measures the extent to which tax on labour income discourages employment. This indicator is measured in percentage of labour cost. Note that the tax wedge is commonly presented for single and childless workers.
Source: OECD Taxing Wages (2020).

2.2. Informal work

Informal, undeclared work involves workers (and their employers) who do not declare part of their earnings, or do not declare their earnings at all. In the absence of taxation of labour income, those engaged in informal and undeclared work will have higher take-home pay than otherwise similar workers, but this comes at a price. Informal work is not covered by social protection arrangements in the area of health, unemployment and pensions.

Often, the undeclared work constitutes a de facto direct employment relationship between a household and an informal service provider. However, these arrangements usually operate in absence of formal employment contracts and outside of national regulatory frameworks (European Commission, 2015[12]). Furthermore, those who do not declare at all, such as illegal immigrants or status holders without work-permit, are exposed to substantial risks of exploitation and sub-standard working conditions. Then again, for many of the migrants, informal employment is frequently the only option of employment as official working permits are often out of reach. In the very short term, engaging in informal employment, or not declaring a limited part of earnings, may not hold involve much risk for workers. However, protracted work under informal and precarious employment conditions leads to an accumulation of disadvantage in the longer term (Ramos Martin and Ruiz, 2020[13]). On the other hand, employers of informal workers are also exposed to increased risk; particularly as such employment is considered illegal in many countries and may be subject to substantial penalties.

While obtaining detailed information on formal non-care household service provision is complicated, it is even more difficult to get a good overview of employment in the undeclared household service sector, as by its very nature these services are not recorded by national labour, tax or statistical agencies. One way of estimating the size of informal employment is to use ISCO data on occupations in conjunction with household expenditure data as in the Classification of Individual Consumption According to Purpose

(COICOP). Among other things, these data measure expenses on non-care household services in category 05.6.2 *("Domestic services and household services")* and, importantly, regardless of whether these services are provided by declared or undeclared workers. Making assumptions on working hours and price levels, Lebrun (2021[14]) uses this data to estimate the share of undeclared work in non-care household services, by subtracting employment levels based ISCO data from the total employment levels based on COICOP data.

Based on this measurement approach, Figure 2.3 suggests that undeclared work is widespread across Europe: on average European countries, about 57% non-care housework appears to be provided informally. For some countries, such as Belgium with 13% and France with 35%, the extent of undeclared work in the non-care household service sector appears comparatively low, while in for example, Germany and Finland more 75% of work in the sector appears to be informal. Lebrun (2021[14]) notes that these estimates fall into the vicinity of his separate estimates based on Eurobarometer responses, with the exception of a few countries, such as Belgium.

These data have to be interpreted with caution, as they occasionally do not align with other estimates in the literature. For some countries, these estimates seem to be corroborated by other sources. For France, Crédoc (2017[15]) estimated that about 20% of all household service work was undeclared, while Enste (2019[8]) put the share of undeclared work among non-care household services in Germany at almost 90%.

Figure 2.3. Estimated undeclared employment in the non-care household service sector (COICOP)

Share of undeclared work in the non-care household sector based on ISCO data on employment in occupations and non-care household service expenses in the COICOP, 2015

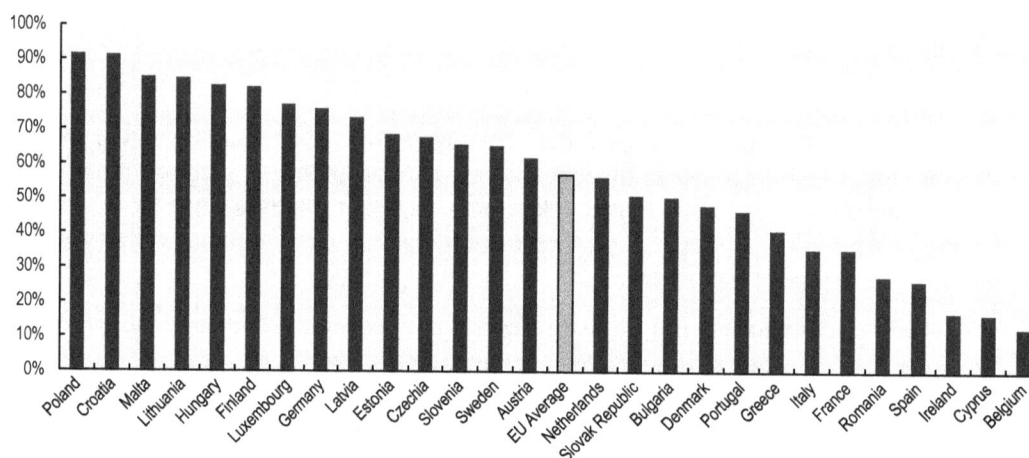

Note: Based on assumptions on working hours and price levels, this approach subtracts ISCO employment levels (code 9 111) from COICOP household expenditure data for non-care household services (code 05.6.2).
Source: Lebrun (2021[14]).

For non-European countries, available estimates often rely on household surveys to assess the population engaging in informal work, rather than the share of informal work among all non-care household service provision. For Canada, for example, 9.2% of respondents to the nationally representative Canadian Survey of Consumer Expectations (CSCE) of the Bank of Canada reported they engaged in informal housecleaning activities between the second and third quarter of 2018 (Kostyshyna and Luu, 2019[16]). For the United States, the nationally representative Survey of Enterprising and Informal Work Activities (EIWA) of the Federal Reserve reported an incidence rate of informal work of about 36% in the general population over the six months prior to respondents completing the survey in 2015. Of these, a share of approximately

27% engaged in informal property maintenance services, such as cleaning, painting, house sitting, yard work and landscaping (Robles and McGee, 2016[17]).[5] The vast majority of domestic workers do not have any sort of employment contract: Burnham and Theodore (2012[18]) suggested it concerned about 90% of domestic workers in metropolitan areas of the United States.

2.3. Platform work

Digital platforms have emerged in the intersection of households and service workers over recent years (Box 2.1). In order to facilitate matching by directly connecting demand and supply of services, these platforms have increasingly created online marketplaces in which workers offer and households buy services (Holts et al., 2019[19]). By providing standardised contracts and vetting potential employees, platforms typically ease the administrative burden for households. However, while digital platforms can improve the efficiency of the matching process, this often comes at the expense of reduced social protection for workers, resulting from common classification as self-employed workers. Also, with increased flexibility of work, owing to their employment status and the short time-frame of most work arrangements ("gig jobs"), service providers often face income volatility, with remuneration frequently falling below minimum wages (Ad-PHS, 2020[20]).

Box 2.1. Regulating platform work

In recent years, the lack of adequate regulation of novel online platforms for service work has received increased attention from policy makers and the public alike. One issue is that even though platform workers share some characteristics with traditional employees, platforms often classify their service providers as self-employed or independent contractors.* This can negatively affect the rights, benefits and labour protections available to platform workers. Platforms often insist that they are merely intermediaries that provide a matchmaking infrastructure. However, it is hard to argue that clients, who buy the services for very short durations, should be considered as legal employers.

In order to improve the conditions for platform workers, some countries have taken legislative action. Since 2017, Portugal grants platform workers with simplified and expedited court proceedings in order to challenge their employment status with the platform. In another case, California implemented the Assembly Bill 5 in January 2020, which put the burden of proof on whether or not a platform service provider is an independent contractor or not on the platform itself. However, with ballot initiative Proposition 22 – passed in November 2020, major ride-sharing and delivery platforms won an exemption from this regulation, leading to a baseline classification as independent contractors for their drivers, although these platforms now have to grant minimum wages and better labour protections to workers.

Working conditions of platform workers can also come through collective bargaining. In Denmark, for example, a popular platform for household cleaning services entered a collective agreement with a major national trade union representing unskilled and vocationally trained workers in 2018. As a result, cleaners operating through this platform are entitled to sick pay, holiday allowances and pension contributions.

Note: * Platform workers sometimes can't, for example, freely set their prices, they need to wear uniforms related to the platform and are unable to fully control their tasks. This bears strong resembles to traditional employer-employee relationships. See OECD (2019[21]) for a discussion on tests and criteria for determining employment status.
Source: Lane (2020[22]), Ad-PHS (2020[20])

Holts et al. (2019[19]) ran a number of surveys across Europe in recent years to measure the size of the platform economy. Digital platforms in the non-care household service sector connect households with local cleaners and include larger ones, such as *Helpling* and *Freska*, or smaller ones, like *Batmaid* and *Moppi*. Publicly run platforms also exist, such as the *Haushaltsjob-Börse* (household service job board) of the German *Minijob-Zentrale*, which connects households with marginal employees (*mini-jobbers*).

The estimates in Holts et al. (2019[19]) cover different years for different countries, and do not necessarily differentiate between non-care, care and other sectors. Despite not being fully comparable, the country estimates in Figure 2.4 show that a sizeable fraction of the working population provides household services at least once per week via digital platforms. For example, about 12% of the working population in the Czech Republic and Spain report to have offered their household service work on a digital platform, while this was less than 4% for Germany, the Netherlands and Sweden. However, much of the work on digital platforms is supplementary to regular earnings, while the share of full-time platform workers is nowhere above 12% of all platform workers (Holts et al., 2019[19]).

Regardless of the type of work arrangement, employment in the non-care household service sector was hit hard since the onset of the COVID-19 pandemic in early 2020. Many provider organisations were shut-down during lockdowns and many of the jobs held before the pandemic were lost, while those that continued to operate often did so in unsafe and risky environments (Box 2.2).

Figure 2.4. Household service provision on digital platforms

Share of working population providing household service activities at least once per week via digital platforms

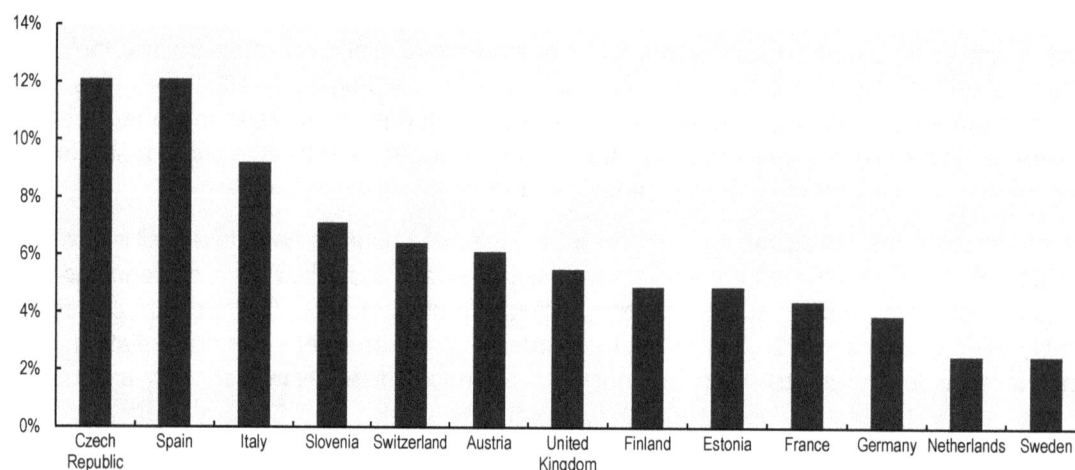

Note: The data was collected via surveys over different years, which may undermine comparability of the data across countries. Data was collected in 2019 for the Czech Republic, France, Slovenia and the United Kingdom; in 2018 for Estonia, Finland and Spain; in 2017 for Italy and Switzerland and in 2016 for Austria, Germany, the Netherlands and Sweden.
Source: Holts et al. (2019[19]).

Box 2.2. COVID-19 and employment in the non-care household service sector

The COVID-19 pandemic has severely affected the workforce worldwide, forcing many to work from home and others to lose their job. The service sector was hit hard as movement was restricted and non-essential businesses were closed. Of the household service organizations in Europe, about a half experienced at least a partial shutdown. At the same time, many household service workers were lacking the same employment protection that was granted to other groups of workers (Ad-PHS, 2020[23]).

Household service workers were often at the risk of job-loss during the pandemic lockdowns, though the impact of the pandemic seems to vary across countries and work arrangements. For example, in France, about a third of all household service provider organisations stopped operations between March and May 2020 (DARES, 2020[24]). In the United States, domestic workers lost more than 90% of their jobs at the onset of the pandemic, leaving up two-thirds without any work by May 2020. The majority of these workers also did not receive any unemployment compensation, leaving many in financial hardship and housing insecurity (NDWA, 2020[25]). In Germany, there were about 12% less workers in marginal employment (Minijobs) in June 2020 compared to the same month of the previous year. Many of those that who lost their employment over this period were household service workers without access to furlough or reduced working hour schemes (Grabka, Braband and Göbler, 2020[26]).

COVID-19 left many household service workers as one of the most exposed groups for workplace transmission of the coronavirus (Lan et al., 2020[27]); informal workers, in particular, faced heightened work- and earnings uncertainty and increased exposure to unsafe workplace conditions (Williams and Kayaoglu, 2020[28]).

3 Unpaid housework

Over years of progress in terms of labour market participation, gender roles regarding domestic house- and care work have remained remarkably rigid (OECD, 2017[29]). However, the traditional model of the male breadwinner and female domestic work is gradually weakening as most working-age women across the OECD are in gainful employment today. However, despite modest increases in male participation in non-care housework tasks, many women in dual-earner or single households still carry out most unpaid work in and around the house (e.g. Bianchi et al. (2000[30]; 2012[31]), Gimenez-Nadal and Sevilla (2012[32]), Sullivan, Billari and Altintas (2014[33]), Gimenez-Nadal and Molina (2020[34])).

Unpaid work generally refers to services that are performed within a household and which are not offered for sale on the market. This typically includes, cooking, cleaning, laundry, gardening, adult- and child-care, as well as shopping and related travel activities. However, the boundaries between unpaid work and leisure are often blurry. For example, some might think of cooking as a highly enjoyable activity, while others see it as a tedious chore. Nevertheless, such tasks can typically be classified by considering whether a third person could be remunerated to perform the same activity (Miranda, 2011[35]). With cooking this is clear – whether a person cooks for themselves, for other household members, or for a dinner party with friends – each of these activities could be replaced by hiring a cook or paying for a meal in a restaurant, meal delivery or takeout. It is therefore considered as unpaid work, rather than pure leisure.

3.1. The distribution of unpaid housework

The OECD Time-Use database provides a picture of the time adults spend on a range of activities, including unpaid work (OECD, 2020[36]). Even if not perfectly comparable across countries as years differ – surveys are expensive and many countries hold them once every 10 years, and important nuances in the measurement and categorisations of activities exist, the data do facilitate the cross-national comparison of time spent on paid and unpaid work.[6] Among all unpaid activities, *non-care housework* makes up the largest share of time in unpaid work. This includes re-occurring non-care tasks in the household, such as cleaning, cooking, laundry, and gardening. Importantly, many of these tasks could be outsourced to household service workers. Nevertheless, in OECD member countries, each day individuals spend on average about 8% of their available time on these tasks (116 minutes), while paid work or study make up 18% per day (262 minutes; note that this accounts for holidays, weekends, part-time work, inactivity etc.) (Figure 3.1). About 6% per day (79 minutes) is spent on other unpaid work, such as shopping, adult- and child-care, as well as travel related to household activities.

Considering the overall time spent on different activities masks substantial differences in time-use that exist among men and women. While men spend about 22% of their time (311 minutes) in paid work or study, women only do so for 15% of their day (213 minutes). Each day, 11% of women's total available time (158 minutes) is spent on non-care housework tasks, while men only spent 5% of their time (72 minutes) on these activities. This culminates in a 6 percentage point (86 minute) gap in time spent on non-care housework on average across the OECD. Figure 3.1 shows that this *Non-Care Housework Gender Gap* varies considerably across countries: it exceeds 13 percentage points in Turkey, where traditional gender norms remain strong (Kagnicioglu, 2017[37]), and is as low as 2 percentage points in Sweden, where gender equality norms have a long history (Evertsson, 2014[38]). While affecting both men and women, the COVID-19 pandemic appears to have had a profound impact on the gender division of unpaid housework across the OECD (see Box 3.1).

Figure 3.1. Time spent on non-care housework across the OECD

Minutes spent on paid and unpaid work in the OECD and gender gap in time spent on non-care housework, 15-64 year-olds, latest available data*

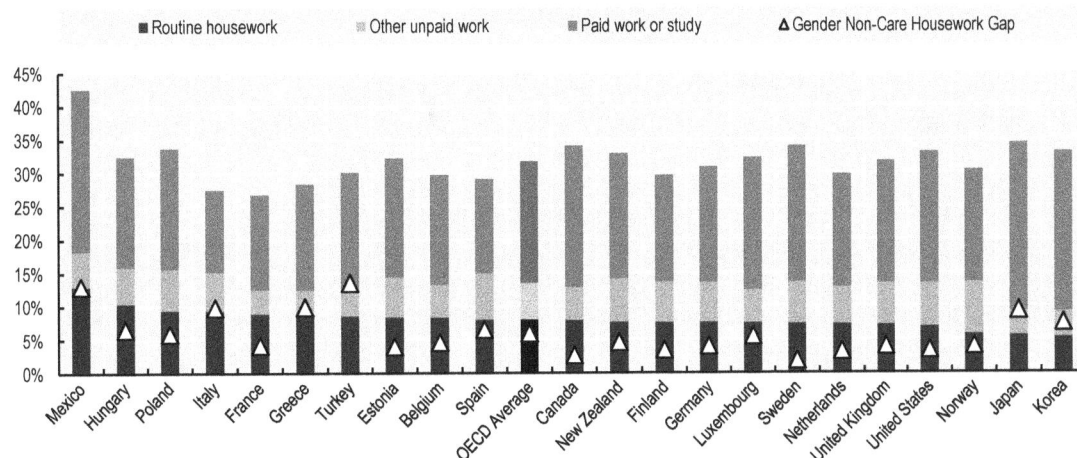

Note: Non-care housework is here defined to concern the following re-occurring non-care tasks in a household (defined as non-care housework in the OECD Time-Use Database): cleaning, cooking, laundry, and gardening. Oher unpaid work refers to care, shopping, volunteering and travel related to unpaid household activities. The Gender Non-Care Housework Gap is calculated by subtracting the male time-use of non-care housework from the female equivalent. Data refers to time-use of 15 to 64-year-olds. Countries for which time-use survey data is older than 2010 are not shown here. Data refer to 2018 for the United States, to 2016 for the Netherlands, to 2015 for Canada, Turkey and the United Kingdom, to 2014 for Italy, Korea and Mexico, to 2013 for Belgium, Germany, Greece, Luxembourg and Poland, to 2011 for Norway and to 2010 for Estonia, Finland, France, Hungary, New Zealand, Spain and Sweden. Time-use categories are not always fully overlapping between countries. Exact groupings and definitions can be obtained through the OECD Time-Use Database in the OECD Gender Data Portal.
Source: OECD calculations based on OECD Time-Use Database.

Even though many women are in gainful employment today, their disproportionate share in unpaid work makes it less likely for them to spend time in paid work compared to men. Across countries, women engage more in the labour market as their male partners take on more housework and less inequality in the distribution of housework between partners is linked to more equality in the labour market (OECD, 2017[29]; 2017[1]).

Box 3.1. COVID-19 and unpaid housework

With worldwide school and childcare facility closures and important shifts to teleworking arrangements, the COVID-19 pandemic affected the amount of housework, its distribution within families, and, perhaps, long-term attitudes towards unpaid housework.

In Italy and Spain, for example, most of the additional unpaid work burden fell on women, even though men increased their contribution too (Del Boca et al., 2020[39]; Farré et al., 2020[40]). This particularly concerned women's involvement in non-care housework, which disproportionately increased relative to that of men. Unpaid house work also increased in the United Kingdom and the Unites States, but evidence as to whether that led to more egalitarian sharing is mixed (Carlson, Petts and Pepin, 2020[41];

Hupkau and Petrongolo, 2020[42]; Oreffice and Quintana-Domeque, 2020[43]; Xue and McMunn, 2021[44]).

Even if the additional housework burden is on average equally shared between men and women, the pandemic may affect views towards the division of housework within households as well as the distribution of this division across the population. For example, in Germany, the housework burden increased by about an hour for each household and was equally shared between men and women (Zinn, 2020[45]; Kreyenfeld et al., 2020[46]; Hipp and Bünning, 2020[47]). However, because of substantial imbalance in the distribution of housework prior to the pandemic, most women judged the overall division as unfair, while two-thirds of men thought the opposite (Bertelsmann Stiftung, 2020[48]). At the same time, in Germany, the pandemic has moved some households towards extremes of the gender housework distribution, either traditional housework roles in which women take on almost all unpaid housework or role reversals where men take on the majority of unpaid housework (Hank and Steinbach, 2020[49]).

Despite the increased burden for women in many countries, men *generally* increased their contribution to housework during the pandemic, albeit from an often low base. In the long term, this may shift gender norms around unpaid work as men have become more exposed to the burden of domestic work and primary caregiving (Alon et al., 2020[50]; Hupkau and Petrongolo, 2020[42]).

3.2. The economic value of unpaid housework

Without household work, households would not function, but despite its significance, housework typically remains unpaid and its economic value therefore elusive. In general, household members carry out the housework themselves and the process does not involve any monetary exchange, prices and/or wages. Nonetheless, any decision on cleaning, cooking or doing the laundry explicitly or implicitly weighs the costs of outsourcing against the efforts of own-account housework – a fundamental economic decision. While costs are a significant barrier to housework outsourcing, other barriers, such as availability, quality and reliability of service provision are also important (Williams, Windebank and Nadin, 2012[51]). The decision on whether or not outsource housework cannot simply be related to relative prices.

Measuring the economic value of housework is key to understanding the importance of unpaid domestic work and the associated opportunity costs. Such valuations measure the total economic contribution of housework and therefore the accumulated value of the domestic work men and women perform within their households. Past work by van de Ven, Zwijnenburg and De Queljoe (2018[52]) and Ahmad and Koh (2011[53]) estimated the economic value of overall housework in selected countries, and this report follows and refines these approaches (the text below outlines the main estimation approach and deviations from previous studies).

By and large, the estimates are generated using the OECD National Accounts and OECD Time-Use data, along with a small number of other OECD datasets (see the notes to Figure 3.2). This report focusses on non-care housework, and thus shifts the focus from unpaid work in general, to the most significant activity therein (see Figure 3.1). A critical component in estimating the economic contribution of non-care housework is the method of valuing the time spent on these activities. Housework can be outsourced to household service providers that relieve household members from these tasks against a price on their labour, thereby creating employment opportunities and economic value. One could thus assume that one hour of unpaid housework would be as valuable as the price of the same hour of housework bought from non-care household service providers (Box 3.2). Time spent on housework is also time potentially foregone in paid employment or leisure. As such, domestic work also holds significant opportunity costs, as the benefits of freed up time – be it through increased income from paid work or well-being – can be substantial. A second approach therefore estimates the market income foregone as a result of engaging in unpaid housework. Importantly, both approaches do not differentiate between the value each man or woman contributes, neither in productivity nor in the value of each hour of work provided, but rather accumulate the total amount of housework performed in a given country (of which women generally provide a larger share).

Box 3.2. Valuing unpaid housework activities

In valuing unpaid work activities, two different approaches of valuation are typically used: one based on replacement costs, the other on opportunity costs. These approaches involve different assumptions on wages and associated tax rates, and thus lead to substantially different results:

- **Replacement Cost Approach:** This approach constructs a post-tax hourly price for housework activities, based on representative prices for similar activities in the market. In particular, the hourly valuation is based on the average of OECD Purchasing Power Parity survey data for non-care household service activities, specifically for registered and unregistered domestic cleaners as well as cleaning companies. In practice, this comes close to using minimum wages as an approximated value of housework. This approach ignores productivity and quality differences between own-account housework and the work of service providers. While these may be substantial, there is no easy way to take such differences into account and the approaches that do so, typically use arbitrary productivity adjustments in their estimates (Landefeld, Fraumeni and Vojtech, 2009[54]). In line with van de Ven, Zwijnenburg and De Queljoe (2018[52]) and Ahmad and Koh (2011[53]), this report assumes productivity differences to be non-existent.

- **Opportunity Cost Approach:** This approach constructs a post-tax hourly price for housework activities, based on the average hourly net wage paid throughout the whole economy. This approximates foregone market income when spending time in unpaid housework. In the absence of detailed household level information on hourly net wages, the economy-wide average wage is an approximation, assuming households can fully compensate saved time with gainful employment.

The full estimation framework requires further assumptions on relevant tax rates and social security contributions. The tax rates used here are from the *OECD Tax-Benefit Model* (version 2.3.0), which offers detailed tax information for various different households constellations (OECD, 2020[55]). In general, the replacement cost approach uses tax rates based on incomes at the lower end of the wage spectrum, while the opportunity cost approach is based on households earning average wages.*

While housework predominately requires labour input, a range of household appliances can substitute or reduce labour input, such as washing machines, dishwashers, microwaves, and others. In particular for women in developed countries, Heisig (2011[56]) shows that technological advances have reduced the time spent on housework. Even though the impact on outcomes is usually small, these appliances therefore need to be adequately reflected in the calculation of the value of own-account production of unpaid non-care housework activities. Under assumptions on the average service life of household appliances, depreciation rates and returns on invested capital, the value of household appliances can be estimated using the Perpetual Inventory Method (PIM) and the OECD National Accounts Data on household consumption expenditure. This report follows the previous approaches of van de Ven, Zwijnenburg and De Queljoe (2018[52]) and Ahmad and Koh (2011[53]) insofar that the capital services considered are based on the following items from the Classification of Individual Consumption According to Purpose (COICOP): household appliances (P31CP053) as well as tools and equipment for house and garden (P31CP055). In contrast to these previous approaches however, purchases of vehicles (P31CP071) are excluded.

Note: * The tax rates for the *replacement cost approach* are based on the average rates for four model households: a single person at 67% of average earnings and no child; a single person at 67% of average earnings with two children; a two-earner married couple with 2 children, both parents with 67% of average earnings; and, a two-earner married couple with no children, both parents with 67% of average earnings. The tax rates in the *opportunity cost approach* are based on two model households: A single person at 100% of average earnings and no child; as well as a two-earner married couple with two children, one parent at 100% of average earnings and the other at 100%.

Because of the need for underlying assumptions, the resulting estimates need to be interpreted with care and therefore do not fully reflect the real value of housework. In addition, given likely productivity differences between own-account and market production of housework and potential capacity limits in the substitution of time spent on housework with time in gainful employment, the estimates from both the "replacement cost and opportunity cost approaches" may overestimate the economic value of housework. Therefore, all results need to be considered as indicative figures that highlight the importance of unpaid non-care housework for the economy. Figure 3.2 presents estimates on the total value of own-account production of unpaid housework activities in 2018. Both approaches point to the substantial economic value of unpaid housework. The replacement cost method values unpaid housework activities at about 15% of GDP on average across available OECD countries, while the opportunity cost method points to a value of 27% of GDP. The latter method generates limited variation in values – especially among European countries (except Luxembourg, Poland, and Sweden), at around 30% of GDP. As household service prices differ more strongly across countries, there is more variation using the replacement cost method, ranging from 23% Greece and Spain to 8% in Luxembourg. Given that housework is only one part of unpaid work (though by far the largest), the estimates are somewhat lower than the figures in van de Ven, Zwijnenburg and De Queljoe (2018[52]) and Ahmad and Koh (2011[53]), both of which consider all unpaid work.

Nevertheless, the results indicate the importance of unpaid non-care housework. Under the replacement cost approach, the GDP-share of the value created by cooking, cleaning, ironing, gardening and small repairs is, for example, almost as large as the average value added by the manufacturing sector (OECD, 2021[57]).

Non-care housework is unequally distributed among men and women. Hence, Figure 3.2 shows that for both approaches women provide a larger share of the value of housework than men: On average, two-thirds of the total value is contributed by women. There are considerable cross-national differences: the value of male housework is almost as large as the value of female housework in countries with high gender quality, such as Sweden, but only concerns 10% of women's contribution in countries with stronger division in gender roles.

The estimates illustrate that women currently create more economic value through unpaid housework than men, and that they would gain much more than men from outsourcing housework to household service providers. Valuing housework is not just an issue of putting a monetary value on an unpaid activity, but also one of considering equality of opportunity in the labour market.

Figure 3.2. The economic contribution of non-care housework

Value of own-account production of unpaid non-care housework activities (% of GDP), 2018

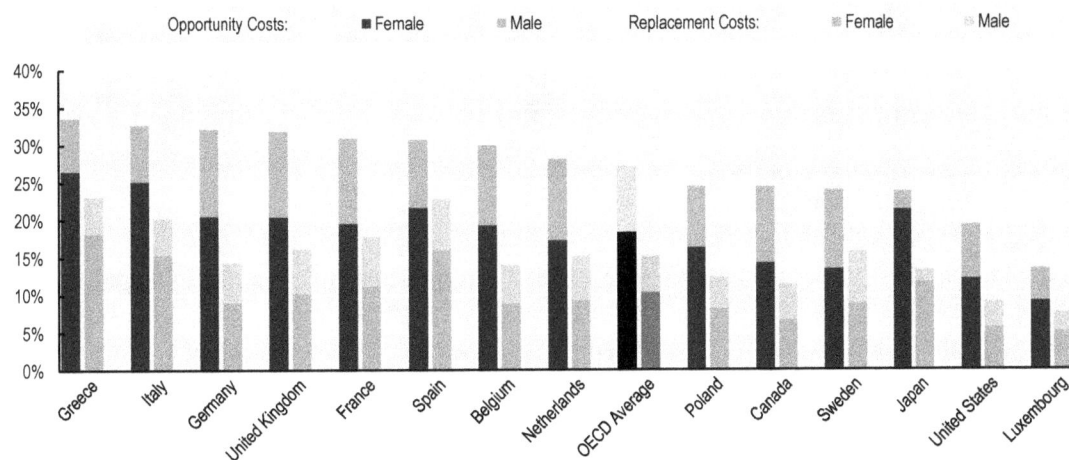

Note: All calculations are based on van de Ven, Zwijnenburg and De Queljoe (2018[52]) as well as Ahmad and Koh (2011[53]). The *Replacement Cost Approach* constructs a post-tax hourly price for housework activities, based on representative prices for similar activities in the market. The *Opportunity Cost Approach* constructs a post-tax hourly price for housework activities, based on the average hourly net wage paid throughout the whole economy. The computations use the latest available time-use data. In the absence of 2018 data for the majority of countries, the calculations thus employ historical time-use statistics. Countries for which time-use survey data is older than 2010 or for which one of the methods cannot be computed (e.g. due to missing data) are not displayed here. The time-use refers to 2018 for the United States, to 2016 for the Netherlands, to 2015 for Canada and the United Kingdom, to 2014 for Italy, to 2013 for Belgium, Germany, Greece, Luxembourg and Poland, and to 2010 for France, Hungary, Spain and Sweden. Time-use categories are not always fully overlapping between countries. Exact groupings and definitions can be obtained through the OECD Time-Use Database in the OECD Gender Data Portal.
Source: OECD calculations based on the OECD Time-Use Database, the OECD Taxing Wages Database, the OECD Tax-Benefit Model, OECD National Accounts Statistics and OECD Purchasing Power Parities.

4 International approaches to household service formalisation

With the goal of increasing work-life balance for households – particularly for women in employment – and reducing the wide-ranging practice of undeclared employment, a number of countries across the OECD have implemented policies to formalise and boost the non-care household service sector. By subsidising formal non-care household services (reducing both consumer prices and increasing take-home pay) and easing administrative procedures, policy interventions make the use of formal non-care household services more attractive to households. Facilitating the outsourcing of housework intends to increase the labour force participation of women, who carry out most unpaid housework, but objectives also include creating new job opportunities for low-skilled workers and the (long-term) unemployed.

This section reviews different approaches to formalising household services in the OECD by introducing some more or less comprehensive household service policy systems in Belgium, Finland, France, Germany and Sweden. The design of policies is considered as well as their implications for the size of the undeclared sector, employment in the non-care service sector, and the quality of work. Other European countries also have relevant policies, but these are usually less comprehensive and not discussed in detail (a brief non-exhaustive overview over some of their policy frameworks is available in Annex A). Non-European OECD countries generally have less developed policy frameworks that mainly centre around working permit programmes for live-in care workers, such as in Korea and Canada (with the exception of the province of Québec, see Annex A). In the United States there is no specific policy towards formalisation of the (non-care) household service market, and here undocumented migrants often carry out work on an informal basis (Jokela, 2017[58]).

Table 4.1 presents the main policy instruments as operational in Belgium, Finland, France, Germany and Sweden. The fiscal aspects of the different instruments are calculated assuming a two-adult household with two dependent children that pools the available deductions and social vouchers as shown in national currency as well as 2019 USD Purchasing Power Parities (PPPs). The bottom part of the table pools the instruments together and highlights the total available subsidy, which is the sum of all available household service tax deductions at the maximum threshold and the maximum social vouchers volume. The cost reduction at maximum subsidy is the share of total expenses subsidised by the government when reaching the tax deduction ceiling or buying the maximum amount of social vouchers available per household.

Table 4.1. Overview of main policy instruments in five countries

		Belgium[2]	Finland[3]	France[4]	Germany[5]	Sweden[6]
Main policy instrument		Social voucher, tax credit	Tax credit	Social voucher, tax credit	Tax credit	Tax credit
Name		Titres services / Dienstencheque	Kotitalousvähennys	CESU, Crédit d'impôt pour l'emploi à domicile	Steuerermäßigung für haushaltsnahe Dienstleistungen	RUT-Avdrag
Operating agencies		Regional governments, Sodexo, Belgian Tax Administration	Finnish Tax Administration	URSSAF (+ private contractors), French Tax Administration	German Tax Agency	Swedish Tax Agency
Covered services		Non-care	Non-care, care & renovation	Non-care & care	Non-care, care & renovation	Non-care & care
Work arrangements		Tripartite	Tri- & bipartite	Tri- & bipartite	Tri- & bipartite	Tripartite
Provider types		Provider organisations (for- & non-profit) Micro-enterprises	Provider organisations (for- & non-profit, public) Direct employment	Direct employment Provider organisations (for- & non-profit) Micro-enterprises	Provider organisations (for- & non-profit) Direct employment	Provider organisations (for-profit) Micro-enterprises
Public Spending (GDP)	Total	0.48% (2017)	0.21% (2019)	0.31% (2014)	0.08% (2019)	0.11% (2017)
	Non-care	0.48% (2017)	~0.06% (2019)	0.18% (2014)	~0.02% (2019)	~0.10% (2017)
Workers	Total	150 000 (2019)	4 900 (2012)	1 300 000	~370 000 (2018)	21 686 (2019)
	Non-care	150 000 (2019)	/	/	/	/
Tax credit	Applicable to	Voucher costs	Labour costs[3]	Labour costs	Labour costs	Labour costs
	Rate	10-20% (varying by region)	40% (service provider) 15% (direct emp.)[3]	50%	20%	50%
	Tax claims	Non-refundable	Non-refundable	Refundable	Non-refundable	Non-refundable
	Reporting	Tax return (annual)	Tax return (annual) Tax card (immediate)	Tax return (annual)	Tax return (annual)	Through provider (immediate)
	Max. credit	EUR 440 PPP 581	EUR 4 500 PPP 5 332	EUR 7 500 PPP 10 267	EUR 4 000[5] PPP 5 386[5]	SEK 75 000 PPP 8 448
Social voucher	Price & value	EUR 9 / 10 (800 / 200 vouchers) exchangeable for 1h of work (EUR 23.50 / PPP 31)	/	Pre-specified by issuer	/	/
	Paid by	Households	/	Employers Local authorities Social organisations	/	/
	Maximum net value	EUR 14 300 PPP 18 869	/	EUR 3 660 PPP 5 010	/	/
Total subsidies[1]	Maximum annual subsidy	EUR 14 740 PPP 19 450	EUR 4 500 PPP 5 331	EUR 11 160 (or 14 801)[4] PPP 15 276 (or 20 261)[4]	EUR 4 000 PPP 5 386	SEK 75 000 PPP 8 448
	Cost reduction at maximum subsidy	62.72%[2]	39.65%	59.81% (or 79.32%)[4]	20,00%	50.00%

Notes: Entries indicated with " ~" mark rough estimations based on calculations and assumptions laid out in the following sub-sections, entries marked with" /" indicate statistics that could not be identified by the authors or that specific policy instruments are absent.

1. For all countries calculations are based on maximum available subsidy per year for a two-earner household with two dependent children. That is, the maximum subsidy pools all available tax credits and voucher subsidies at the respective tax credit ceiling or maximum voucher volume. The effective cost reduction at the maximum subsidy calculates the share of total labour costs for household service work reduced through the policies at the maximum subsidy.

2. For Belgium, calculations assume a household in the Brussels region (tax credit of 15% on first 163 vouchers; value of voucher EUR 23.50 / PPP 31). The effective cost reduction higher for lower voucher volumes (1-300: 68%; 301-800: 64%). The number of workers refer to employees in the sector in the fourth quarter of 2019.

3. For Finland, the effective cost reduction is lower for direct employment (14.9%). For direct employment, the tax credit applies to the wage costs, while employer contributions are 100% covered.

4. For France, the housework share is solely based on services provided through tripartite modes. The declarative CESU voucher eases administrative access and additional social security exemptions of 2 EUR (PPP 2.73) per hour of work are available for direct employment. Therefore, the maximum annual subsidy for France depends on the nature of the service provision. In the case of direct domestic employment, the maximum subsidy increases by PPP 4 9 185 (calculated assuming a minimum wage). This higher value is presented in parenthesis.

5. For Germany, marginal employees (earning less than EUR 450, or PPP 606, per month or work less than 3 months or 70 days per year) are exempt from income taxation. A household voucher eases their employment. The German tax credit has a lower deduction ceiling for renovation work, i.e. EUR 1 200 (PPP 1 615)

6. For Sweden, the total subsidy together with the ROT-reduction cannot exceed SEK 75 000 (PPP 18 448). The RUT-deduction can also be applied to direct domestic employment, but in this case, it only applies to the employer contributions and not to the wages paid. As such, RUT-subsidised direct employment is relatively rare and thus excluded from this overview.

4.1. Policy objectives

While most household service policy systems aim at formalising the sector, the underlying mix of objectives may differ, but generally also includes improving job-opportunities for the low skilled and enhancing their social protection coverage as well as easing work/life balance issues within families. As one of the first comprehensive policy frameworks, the French Government introduced in the early 1990s tax credits for domestic employment, the *Crédit d'impôt pour l'emploi à domicile*, and two social vouchers, *Chèque Emploi Service* and *Titre Emploi-Service*, which could be used to pay personal and household services. The main motivation behind formalising the sector was to increase employment levels among the lower qualified as well as providing support for the elderly (Guiraudon and Ledoux, 2015[59]). Both vouchers were replaced by the universal social *Chèque emploi service universel* (CESU) system in 2006, which comprises the *pre-financed CESU,* a social voucher, and the *declarative CESU,* a simplified declaration and remuneration system for directly employed domestic workers.

After running initial regional pilot trials across the country from 1997, Finland introduced the Domestic Help Service Tax Credit (DHSTC), called *Kotitalousvähennys*, in 2001. Besides increased formalisation of the household service sector, the main objective of this framework was to increase the work-life balance within families and to boost employment among lower-qualified population segments (Aalto, 2015[60]).

Since 2003, the German Government grants a tax credit on household services, called *Steuerermäßigung für haushaltsnahe Dienstleistungen*. The objective of this system is an expansion of employment in the household service sector, which traditionally faced labour shortages. Along with the tax credit, and overall large-scale labour market reforms in the same year, the government also introduced the concept of *Minijobs* (marginal employment) and *Haushaltsschecks (*household cheques), aimed at greatly simplifying small-scale (domestic) employment. With an extension of the tax credit in 2005, the focus of the policy framework was shifted to encompass support for mothers and dual-earner families (Shire, 2015[61]).

In 2004, Belgium implemented a comprehensive system of social vouchers on the non-care household service market, called *Titres services* or *Dienstencheque*. With a primary objective of incentivising the consumption and provision of declared services, the system was also designed to offer new employment opportunities with better social protection coverage to lower qualified workers. Since then, the motivation for the social vouchers has shifted to some degree, so that they are currently seen more as a middle-class tax break that enables better work-life balance and more employment chances for higher qualified women (Marx and Vandelannoote, 2015[62]; Raz-Yurovich and Marx, 2018[63]).

The Swedish Government introduced the *RUT-Avdrag* in 2007, in order to tackle the high tax wedge for domestic household services and to boost formal employment in this sector, along with increasing female employment more generally by reducing time-stress associated with routine household tasks. Over the years and with a large influx of asylum seekers, the RUT-deduction recently has been regarded as a tool for the labour market integration of refugees (Rickne, 2019[64]).

4.2. Policy instruments

Governments can use different tools to formalise the non-care household service sector. Usually governments choose demand-side measures, such as tax credits and social vouchers, but favourable tax treatment can also include reduced VAT-rates and reduced employer social security contributions. Each of these instruments may be used in isolation, but often the non-care household service sector is supported by a combination of instruments. As such, some countries have complex systems that involve multiple actors and instruments.

Most of the policy instruments work by reducing the effective prices for formal household service work. With lower prices, the consumption of undeclared services is supposed to decrease as the incentives for this form of employment weaken. However, price levels are not the only consideration for either household or service providers. Policies can also aim to ease access to the services and simplify employment formalities.

4.2.1. Tax credits

Tax credits serve as a tool to reduce net service prices, by granting a deduction on the annual tax liability of households that use non-care household services, relative to the volume of service work consumed and up to a certain threshold – a tax deduction ceiling. National tax authorities operate these instruments.

Tax credits may be the preferred mode for delivering social support as they are often seen as tax cuts, and, for example in the United States, tax cuts are likely to be more palatable to policy makers and the general public rather than increased government spending on welfare programmes (Forman, 2010[65]; Ashok and Huber, 2020[66]).

Of the countries presented in Table 4.1, each one has some form of tax credit towards the cost of buying household services, but the design of tax credits varies considerably across countries in terms of value and ceilings of tax deductions. The largest tax credits can be found in Sweden and France, where governments grant a deduction of 50% on the labour costs for household service work, up to a deduction ceiling of SEK 75 000 (PPP 8 448) and EUR 7 500 (PPP 10 267) per household, respectively. In Finland, the tax incentives differ between work arrangements and only apply to costs above EUR 100 (PPP 118) per year: the tax credit is 40% on the labour costs for services purchased through provider organisations, but only 15% on the wages for directly employed domestic workers, along with 100% on all employer contributions. In both cases, the maximum reimbursement amounts to EUR 4 500 (PPP 5 332) per household. Germany grants a tax credit of 20%, up to a deduction ceiling of EUR 4 000 (PPP 5 386) for household services or EUR 1 200 (PPP 1 615) for renovation work. As laid out in Annex A, similar tax credits exists in, for example, Denmark (*BoligJobordningen)* and Luxembourg (*Abattement pour charges extraordinaires*). The Belgian tax credit differs from those in other countries as it only applies to the cost of the service vouchers themselves. The level of the deduction and the reimbursement ceiling varies across the Belgian regions (see below).

Refundability of tax credits

Tax credits generally only **benefit** those **households with sufficiently** large incomes and tax liabilities – i.e. the tax credit is "wasteable" or non-refundable. Low-income households may not earn enough to pay tax and thus do not benefit from the tax credit, or their tax liability is so small that they cannot benefit from the tax credit in full. To overcome this issue and bolster fairness in programme design, tax credits can be made "non-wasteable" or refundable: low-income households receive a cash payment of equivalent value to the tax credit made to richer households who offset the tax-credit to their tax liabilities. Most countries only have non-refundable tax credits for household services Table 4.1, France is the only one that currently grants refundable tax credits (see Box 4.1).

Box 4.1. The French household service tax credit and social voucher system

Since 1991, the French Government grants a refundable tax credit of 50% for household service work, up to an expense ceiling of EUR 15 000 (PPP 20 534), depending on the number of dependent children in the household.* Thus, tax-paying households can be reimbursed up to EUR 7 500 (PPP 10 267). Initially, the tax credit was introduced as non-refundable, though between 2007 and 2016 the French tax code was amended, such that households in employment would receive a tax refund, even if their tax liability was smaller than the applicable reimbursement. In 2017, the refundability of the tax credit was generalised to all households with a further amendment of the tax code.

The additional French Universal Service Voucher (CESU), available either as a declarative system or a social voucher,, is applicable to a wide range of activities inside and outside of the consumer's household.** With its creation in 2006, along with precursors from the early 1990s, it aims to formalise the (household) service sector and to increase the work-life balance of employees and their families. As such, the two different types of CESU follow somewhat different objectives and mechanisms and are managed by different private contractors:***

- The *declarative CESU* aims to simplify the direct employment of service providers in a household by enabling households to declare their workers through the CESU. This declaration automatically generates payslips when households indicate the number of working hours, wages and bonuses to be paid. For the employee, it guarantees rights to health insurance, unemployment benefits and pension. Since 2020, the newly introduced CESU+ also allows for direct handling of salaries with automatic transfers from bank accounts declared on the CESU+ platform.

- The *prefinanced CESU* is a social voucher of a predefined value, paid for and distributed by employers to their employees, who can use them to pay for various service work (fully or in part). Each employee can receive vouchers up to a value of EUR 1 830 (PPP 2 505) per year, while employers can claim a tax reduction of 25% up to a ceiling of EUR 500 000 (PPP 684 450) against the costs of the vouchers. In addition, employers are also exempt from social security contributions on the value spent on the vouchers for their employees. In contrast to the declarative CESU, the prefinanced voucher can also be used pay for services through provider organisations. Both local authorities and insurances can also distribute prefinanced vouchers to distribute social allowances (social CESU).

In addition to tax credits and social vouchers, French households additionally benefit from an exemption of EUR 2 (PPP 2.74) per hour worked on employment contributions for their domestic employees if they are directly employed by the household and not through an intermediary.****

In terms of demand-side measures, non-profit service provider organisations benefit from full or partial exemptions from employer contributions as well as reduced VAT rates. Instead of the usual 20%, their household services are taxed at 10% while services to the frail and dependent are taxed at 5.5%.

Notes: * The baseline expense ceiling is EUR 12 000 (PPP 16 427) per household, but EUR 1 500 (PPP 2053) are added for each dependent child in the household. It can be increased to EUR 20 000 (PPP 27 378) in case of a disabled person in the household ** The household services include, among others, cleaning, ironing, gardening, childcare, elderly assistance, maintenance work, tutoring, IT support. *** The declarative CESU is issued by URSSAF, who then handle all administrative tasks of the domestic employment, such as payroll records and social security contributions. The prefinanced CESU is issued by multiple private entities (Domiserve, Edenred, Groupe UP, Natixis Intertitres and Sodexo). **** The exemption on social security contributions was abolished in 2011, but reintroduced in 2015.
Source: Ad-PHS (2020[67]), Williams (2018[68])

With the final generalised refundability of the French tax credit, the public expenditure on the household service sector increased by 15.4% (DARES, 2019[69]). Since the support was made available to more low-income households and the elderly, the number of tax credit claims increased by about 6% compared to 2016, after the number of claims had been relatively stable for some years (DGFiP, 2021[70]). However, the overall number of hours worked in the sector did not change significantly over the same year – if anything they fell by about 2 million (DARES, 2020[71]). Rather than drawing new consumers to the household service market, this suggests that the main effect of reform was to allow for new claims among low-income households and the elderly who already used household services in the absence of tax benefits or those who could only claim a small amount. Making tax credits towards household services refundable may not be particularly effective in reaching entirely new consumers and boosting the overall size of the sector (see e.g. Carbonnier (2015[72]) or Marbot and Roy (2014[73])).

Operational issues

Tax administrations were set up to collect money rather than distribute cash transfers. Embedding "refundability of tax credits" in the operations of tax administrations can introduce a complicated administrative challenge prone to errors (Forman, 2010[65]). In the United States, for example, between 22 and 26% of tax refunds related to the Earned Income Tax Credit are paid out in error, either resulting from errors in the reporting, owing to the complexity of the system, or intentional misreporting (Tax Policy Center, 2020[74]). One issue around income-tested refundable tax credit is to **assess entitlements in a timely manner**, which "[…] involves a series of decisions on what to include as income, whose income in a household is included, over what time period income is measured, how long awards should last, and how responsive the system should be to changes in income and circumstances during the period of the award [.]" (Millar and Whiteford, 2020[75]). Given the different "timing elements" involved, it is easily imagined that payments made can be incorrect, requiring repayment or, instead, supplementary payments at a later stage, all at considerable administrative cost. Furthermore, in an environment, which is strongly focused on "tackling fraud", this can lead to legitimate claims for support to be denied while excessive penalties on alleged wrongdoing can be applied. For example, an investigation by the Dutch Parliamentary commission on the implementation of the childcare supplement by the Dutch tax authorities found that many parents were wrongly branded as deliberate fraudsters (Parlementaire Ondervragingscommissie Kinderopvangtoeslag, 2020[76]).

The **timing of awarding tax credits** is another key issue. Tax credits, like tax liabilities may accumulate over the year and only be granted upon reporting with the annual tax return. This means that users of non-care household services pay for the service upfront and wait for the final annual tax settlement to obtain the relevant amount, as for example in Finland and Germany.[7] While this system is common, it may exclude certain households, as paying upfront may be too expensive for low-income earners. In addition, tax payers are often not fully aware of tax incentives – for example through psychological frictions, such as programme confusion and informational complexity – leading to incomplete take-up of tax credits (Bhargava and Manoli, 2015[77]; Chetty and Saez, 2013[78]).

Instead, **tax credits** can be **"granted at source"** and thus immediately reduce the service prices for consumers. In Sweden, the service fee already accounts for the tax credit, so consumers do not need to cover the subsidy upfront (see Box 4.2). France, which currently operates the household service tax credit through annual tax returns, will grant the tax benefits at source from 2022 (Ministère de l'Action et des Comptes publics, 2021[79]). Such granting at source makes the fee reductions more visible and reduces confusion, which can increase consumptions particularly among low-income households who would find it harder to pay the full service price upfront. Indeed, after the Swedish tax credit was changed to granting of the benefits at source in 2009, the number of consumers almost doubled (Skatteverket, 2011[80]). In addition, consumers tend to under-react to taxes that are not immediately visible and thus, conversely, may have stronger demand responses to granting tax credits at source (Chetty, Looney and Kroft, 2009[81]). However, awarding the tax credit at source requires service providers to undertake the necessary administrative actions. This does not pose insurmountable cost issues for service providers of a certain size, but would be difficult to stomach for small companies or those who work directly for the service user.

Box 4.2. The Swedish RUT-Deduction

The RUT-deduction (*RUT-avdrag*)*, which came into force in 2007, is a non-refundable tax credit for consumers of domestic household services. The tax credit applies to cleaning, maintenance, and laundry services in the household, as well as some other personal care services. The tax credit is generally available for services provided by registered companies or self-employed micro-entrepreneurs.** Households that apply for the RUT-deduction receive a 50% reduction of the service price charged by service providers. The providers then request the difference between the actual payment received from the consumer and total labour costs, including VAT, from the Swedish Tax Authority. As such, the scheme is simple and straightforward for users, though it involves some additional administrative costs for service providers.

The tax credit reduces labour costs by half, up to a yearly maximum deduction ceiling of initially SEK 50 000 (PPP 5 632) for each person, while spouses can pool the deduction to increase the ceiling. In 2016, the ceiling was reduced to SEK 25 000 (PPP 2 834) for individuals below the age of 65, yet was increased to SEK 50 000 (EUR 5 632) again in 2019. Since 2021, the ceiling is set at SEK 75 000 (PPP 8 448).*** It is open to individual customers who are liable for tax in the given year and who hire a registered business, either self-employed or companies, to provide domestic services. These domestic household services need to be carried out in the customer's household and cannot be undertaken by a relative.

Alongside RUT, Sweden grants the 30% *ROT* tax credit for repair and renovation services, up to a yearly deduction ceiling of SEK 50 000 (PP 5 632). Together with the RUT tax credit, the total deduction for both cannot exceed SEK 75 000 (PPP 8 448) per year.

Note: RUT is an acronym for *Renhållning, Underhåll, Tvätt*, which translates to cleaning, maintenance, laundry. ** The RUT-deduction can also be applied to direct domestic employment, but in this case it only applies to the employer contributions and not to the wages paid. As such, RUT-subsidised direct employment is relatively rare. ***
Source: AD-PHS (2020[82]); Skatteverket.

Indeed, when comparing the Swedish and Finish tax credits, which operate in relatively similar national environments, it appears that the RUT-deduction reaches more low-income households (see page Section 4.7). For example, while only 0.4% of Finish households with incomes below EUR 10 000 (PPP 11 849) received tax credits through the DHSTC, about 8% of Swedish households with comparable incomes below SEK 100 000 (PPP 11 264) received a RUT-reduction. As both countries have only small differences in their tax credit rates, and while deduction ceilings are likely not important at these income levels, this difference may well be related to the Swedish RUT-reduction being more easily accessible as it is granted at source.[8]

When designing tax credit schemes, governments also need to be **clear in communicating** the **rules** and **regulations**. In particular, frequent adjustments of tax credit rates and deduction ceilings may confuse households, which can negatively affect the efficacy of the instrument. For example, the Finish Domestic Help Service Tax Credit (DHSTC) has seen frequent adjustments since its implementation in 2001 (see Box 4.3). As a result, Harju et al. (2021[83]) finds that many Finns are unware of the relevant replacement rates and DHSTC ceilings as well as unable to calculate effective net prices accounting for the tax credit. Many recipients therefore frequently also claim less support than what they are entitled to. In particular, there is significant bunching of claims around the maximum credit ceiling, many claims refer to servcies bought up to EUR 4 500 (PPP 5 332), while in reality that amount is the maximum yearly reimbursement. When using a service provider an amount EUR 11 350 (PPP 13 450) could be claimed instead.

Box 4.3. The Finish Domestic Help Service Tax Credit

The Domestic Help Service Tax Credit (*Kotitalousvähennys*) introduced in 2001 is a non-refundable tax credit for domestic household services, including both care and non-care work as well as renovation activities.

The tax credit is available to all individuals with taxable income who do not already receive some form of service voucher or care allowances. It deducts 40% of the labour-costs for household and/or renovation services provided by private agencies, VAT-registered as well as non-profit organisations, or 15% of the wages and all employer social security contributions for directly employed workers. As such, it is available in both tripartite and traditional domestic employment settings, but service organisations are the predominant provider. In both cases, the tax credit only applies to costs above EUR 100 (PPP 118) and below a ceiling of EUR 2 250 (PPP 2 666) per person. Spouses can pool the tax credit, increasing the maximum deduction per household to EUR 4 500 (PPP 5 332). Individuals can claim the tax credit for services performed in their homes, including holiday homes. Work in the homes of their or their spouse's parents or grandparents are also eligible, as long as the claimants themselves pay the costs.

Over recent years, the ceilings and deduction rates have seen much adjustment. For example, between 2009 and 2011 the credit for service consumed through provider organisations was as high as 60% up to a EUR 3 000 (PPP 3 341) ceiling per person.

Note: In addition, the Finish Government introduced a system of Social and Health Care Vouchers for vulnerable citizens, such as the elderly, in 2004. These vouchers are mainly applicable to health and care services using a more market-based mechanism, but can cover non-care household services, as municipalities have discretion over whom they wish to grant the vouchers to, and for what they can be used. Overall, the social voucher system is a very small part of the wider household service policy framework.
Source: Harju et al. (2021[83]); AD-PHS (2020[84]); Hiilamo (2015[85])

4.2.2. Social vouchers

Social vouchers, defined as social benefits entitling recipients to specific goods or services to improve their work life balance (see Ad-PHS (2020[86])), are another tool to promote the use of non-care household services. Such vouchers are usually **transparent and easy to use**, making them attractive to many households in need for support. In Belgium, for example, the voucher takes the form of a cheque that entitles the buyer to exchange it for non-care household service work (Box 4.4). Households can buy the vouchers themselves. In France, employers regularly issue pre-financed CESU vouchers that entitle their employees to exchange them against household service work.

Social vouchers also make it easier to target support to **target support** at population groups with specific needs for household support. For example, the pre-financed CESU voucher mentioned above can also be distributed by French local authorities and insurances to distribute social allowances to households in need (social CESU). In Belgium (and Italy, see Annex A), voucher prices are fixed, and each of the vouchers can be exchanged for one hour of household service work. This makes the costs involved transparent for the user and the underlying benefits are not dependent on claiming through complicated tax returns, which is likely to affect the overall use of household services. With the pre-financed CESU in France, the value of the voucher is set by the issuing employer or local authority and can then be used to pay for services at the market rate. If the price of the services is higher, households have to pay for the difference themselves.

Box 4.4. The Belgian Service Voucher Scheme

The Service Voucher Scheme (*Titres services* or *Dienstencheque*) is a comprehensive voucher system for non-care household services, including cleaning, laundry and ironing, cooking and grocery shopping. Implemented in 2004, the vouchers are only available in a tripartite system for work provided by service provider organisations.

The system is organised in an interplay between multiple actors. Per year, each resident is eligible to purchase up to 500 service vouchers from a private contractor – Sodexo – who issues the vouchers at two prices fixed by the public authorities. The first 400 vouchers are sold for EUR 9 (PPP 11.88), while the remaining 100 vouchers can be bought for EUR 10 (PPP 13.20). The costs of part of the vouchers can be claimed against a tax deduction which varies across the three Belgian regions. It amounts to 15% on the costs of the first 163 vouchers in Brussels, 20% on the first 169 vouchers in Flanders, and 10% on the first 150 vouchers in Wallonia.* Together, the tax deduction and two-tier pricing system create a progressive support system in which households with lower service volume receive a higher average support per hour of service work consumed.

Households can pool the vouchers, raising the number of available vouchers to 1 000 per family. With the use of each voucher, consumers can pay for-profit and non-profit service provider companies for one hour of non-care service work in their household. Service provider companies – who directly employ household service workers eligible to provide these services – get paid a fixed rate, which marginally varies across the Belgian regions. This reimbursement amounts to EUR 23.50 (PPP 31.00) in Brussels, EUR 23.48 (PPP 30.98) in Flanders, and EUR 23.86 (PPP 31.48) in Wallonia.

Note: *The effective prices on the initial vouchers thus differ across regions: EUR 7.65 (PPP 10.09) in Brussels, EUR 7.20 (PPP 9.50) in Flanders, and EUR 8.10 (PPP 10.69) in Wallonia.
Source: AD-PHS (2020[87]); European Commission (2018[88]); Regional Governments of Brussels, Flanders and Wallonia

4.2.3. Declarative systems

An alternative approach involve declarative systems that aim to **simplify administrative processes** regarding direct domestic employment. Such systems establish a contract between service provider and user, and simplify the handling of social contributions and payroll records as these administrative tasks can be outsourced to external system managers. In France, for example, URSSAF, a private contractor, handles all administration regarding direct domestic employment after households fill out a *declarative CESU* form. A similar approach exists in Austria (*Dienstleistungsscheck*), Germany (*Haushaltschecks*) and Italy (*Libretto di famiglia*), where households can use declarations to buy services provided by marginal employees (for Austria and Italy; see Annex A). While such systems ease the process of hiring domestic employees, they do not absolve the household from entering a legal employment relationship that comes with certain obligations in terms of employment conditions and labour protections.

Like social vouchers, such systems also facilitate **targeting of support** at population groups with specific needs for household support. For example, the *Chèque Emploi-Service* in the Canadian province Québec is available to individuals who have experienced a loss of autonomy, such as the elderly or individuals with disabilities (see Annex A). The system, which functions very similar to the French *declarative CESU,* can be used to simplify administrative processes in hiring personal care or none-care housekeeping activities, in conjunction with direct allowances granted to these groups (Boivin, 2017[89]).

4.2.4. Other instruments

There are a number of additional instruments (not covered in Table 4.1) that are used in the household service market. For example, countries can choose to fully or partially exempt actors in the household service market from employer contributions or other levies. In France, households benefit from an exemption of EUR 2 (PPP 2.74) per hour worked on employment contributions for their domestic employees, if they are directly employed by the household and not through an intermediary. A total exemption of these employer contributions is granted to households with members aged 70 or older as well as those with acute care needs. In the Netherlands, households are exempt from all taxes and employer contributions for directly employed care and (non-care) household service workers who work for four days or less per week (see Annex A). In Spain, direct employers of non-care household service workers can benefit from an exemption of 20% or 45% on their employer contributions to social security, depending on the size of the household (see Annex A).

While most measures discussed so far have been demand side measures, either reducing net consumer prices for services or easing the access to services, countries can also choose supply-side measures that reduce the tax burden on service providers. In addition to the comprehensive French policy framework, for example, service provider organisations are granted reduced VAT-rates on a range of their services.

Another approach is to reduce the high tax-burden on household service employees directly, by reducing or completely waiving taxation of their income. Along with potential, though often partial, social insurance coverage (see section 4.5), this incentivises formal employment as the difference between the take-home pay in formal and informal work arrangements decreases. In Germany, for example, the so-called *Mini-jobbers* (marginal employees) with limited earnings are exempt from income taxation (Box 4.5).

Box 4.5. The German marginal employment scheme and household service tax credit

In 2003, the German Government introduced *Mini-jobs*: workers who earn less than EUR 450 (PPP 606) per month on a regular basis, or who work for less than 3 months or 70 days per year are exempt from income taxation. The minimum wage for these workers is EUR 9.50 (PPP 12.80) per hour. Under this scheme, the mini-jobbers are covered by accident insurance through employer contributions, but are exempt from health- and unemployment insurance. Personal contributions towards pension funds (3.7%) are voluntary on an opt-out basis.

Since the introduction of household cheques (*Haushaltsschecks*), hiring marginal employees under this scheme is made relatively easy for households, which functions relatively similar to the French declarative CESU (see above). After providing information on the employing household and the employee, the cheques are submitted to the *Minijob-Zentrale*, who handles the administrative details, including calculation accident insurance contributions. In addition, households can claim a tax reduction of 20% on their expenses on mini-jobbers up to a maximum refund of EUR 510 (PPP 687) per year. For other domestic employment relationships that do not qualify as marginal employment, a 20% tax credit with a ceiling of EUR 4 000 (PPP 5 286) applies for care and non-care household services, as well as EUR 1 200 (PPP 1 616) regarding renovation work.

Source: Ad-PHS (2020[90]).

4.3. Services covered

Within their policy frameworks, countries can cover a range of different household services. Variation in the household services covered by tax credits and/or vouchers can result from different policy objectives and /or target groups and differences in national contexts (Table 4.2). In general, household services can be split into object-centric non-care services, such as cleaning, laundry, cooking, gardening and smaller home maintenance and repair, or person-centric care activities, such as child-minding and support for the elderly and those with disabilities (Baga et al., 2020[3]).

Non-care household services such as cleaning and laundry services are covered in all five countries. When it comes to cooking, the Swedish RUT-deduction is the only instrument that explicitly excludes it from the list of eligible services and the Belgian service vouchers are the only instrument that excludes gardening as well as smaller maintenance and repair work in the household. The Belgian system is also the only one that currently fully excludes care services, while child-minding and care for the elderly and disabled is covered in all other four countries. The French system of household service policies also covers tutoring services, while the Swedish programme covers small-scale help with school homework.

In some cases, other services that are not easily grouped as non-care or care services are covered too: for example, IT services in the household are covered everywhere but Belgium, or transport services of either furniture or vulnerable people, which are only excluded in Finland. Renovation work may be covered by a separate scheme, such as the Swedish ROT-deduction. In contrast to all other schemes, the Finnish DHSTC and the German tax credit encompass renovation work besides household and care services with the household service framework. Given different national needs, Sweden and Finland also cover snow-shovelling services, while Germany allows for this in the context of road cleaning on private property.

Table 4.2. Services eligible within national household service policies

	Belgium	Finland	France	Germany	Sweden
Non-care	Yes	Yes	Yes	Yes	Yes
	Yes	Yes	Yes	Yes	No
	Yes	Yes	Yes	Yes	Yes
	No	Yes	Yes	Yes	Yes
	No	Yes	Yes	Yes	Yes
	Yes	No	Yes	Yes	No
Care	No	Yes	Yes	Yes	Yes
	No	No	Yes	No	Yes[3]
	No	Yes	Yes	Yes	Yes
Other	No	Yes	No	Yes	No
	No	Yes	Yes	Yes	Yes
	Yes[1]	No	Yes[1]	Yes[2]	Yes[2]
	No	Yes	No	Yes	Yes

Notes: The table only considers the household service policies as presented in Table 1. Each country may have other policy frameworks that cover other services, such as the ROT-reduction for renovation work in Sweden. 1. Transport is covered for the elderly and non-independent persons. 2. Transport is covered for moving purposes. 3. Tutoring is only covered for small-scale support with homework of children.

Given the focus on non-care household services, it is important to identify the importance of care-service support within national policies. In the case of Belgium, this is straightforward as the service vouchers only cover non-care service work. In Sweden, approximately 91% of the RUT work are done in cleaning, gardening, and cooking services (Riksrevisionen, 2020[91]), while about 56% of all household service in German households work falls onto non-care tasks (Juncke, Krämer and Weinelt, 2019[92]).The breadth of the services covered through the DHSTC in Finland makes it complicated to compare it to other countries. According to Harju et al. (2021[83]), the majority of the tax credit volume, about two-thirds of all claims, are applied to renovation work, while only about 28% of the total volume is applied to cleaning and housekeeping. In France, DARES (2020[71]) suggests that about one-third of all work in the household service sector concerns non-care services.

4.4. Size of the programmes

Based on the differences in scope and generosity of the policies, as well as national contexts, the total size of the programmes in terms of employment and public spending also differs across countries. For example, systems with higher tax credit rates may attract more households and larger claim volumes than systems with a low tax credit rate, leading to more employment in the sector but also higher public spending. Likewise, a strong subsidy for social vouchers or other policy instruments can weigh heavily on the public budget while strongly boosting the size of the market. A further factor is the scope of services covered within each policy framework, as discussed in the previous sub-section. A narrow set of services eligible for either tax credits or social vouchers may lead to limited employment and relatively low public spending in the sector. Given the differences in scope, however, it is not straightforward to compare national policies and this sub-section highlights indicators on the size of the programmes supporting the use of non-care household services.

4.4.1. Public spending

Since the administration of the service vouchers was delegated to the regions in 2014, there has been no central tracking of the public expenditure on these instruments. Based on separate sources for 2017 however, the Belgian service vouchers scheme is the largest among all countries considered, costing roughly 0.48% of the GDP (see Figure 4.1). Due to the restricted set of eligible services in Belgium, all of this expenditure was on non-care work. Likewise, France, for which the available data is also fairly dated, also has considerably large public spending on fiscal incentives in the household service market (0.31% of GDP in 2014), with non-care services making up about two-thirds of this. The public spending in Finland, Germany and Sweden is lower, with public expenditure on non-care services falling below 0.10% of GDP in each of these countries.

Figure 4.1. Public spending on household service policy instruments

Total public spending on major household service policy instruments as a share of GDP, non-care and other services, latest year available

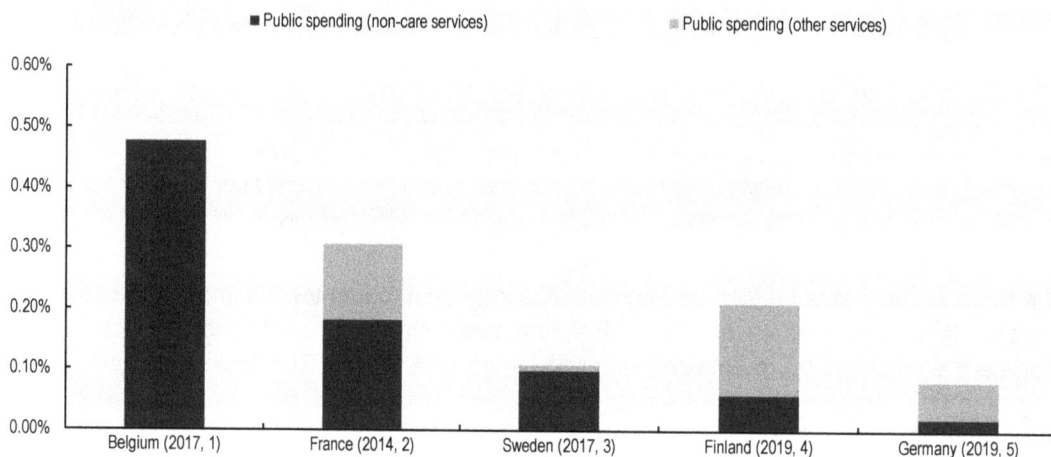

Notes:
1. For Belgium, public spending sums the costs of the service voucher subsidy and the tax credits for service voucher costs.
2. For France, public spending includes fiscal incentives in the household service market, i.e. tax credits, VAT-reductions and exemptions on employer contributions. It excludes about EUR 5 billion of direct aids paid departmental councils and the pension and family allowance funds. About 90% of these expenses are going towards care activities.
3. For Sweden, non-care spending is based on the total expenditure on the RUT-reduction and a back-of-the-envelope calculation using an average price for cleaning services of about SEK 200 per hour (after tax credit) and the fact that 91% of RUT work are performed in non-care household services.
4. For Finland, non-care spending is based on the total DHSTC volume and a back-of-the-envelope calculation extrapolating from survey results in Harju et al. (2021[83]), according to which non-care household services make up 28% of all DHSTC work.
5. For Germany, non-care spending is based on the total expenditure on the German tax credit for household services and a back-of-the-envelope calculation because non-care represents about 56% of all non-renovation household service work provided.
Source: Lebrun and Fourna (2016[93]); OECD calculations based on Vlaamse DWSE (2020[94]), IDEA Consult (2020[95]), Cour des comptes de Belgique (2018[96]), Parlement de Wallonie (2019[97]), Riksrevisionen (2020[91]), Verohallinto (2021[98]) and Bundesminsterium der Finanzen (2019[99]).

4.4.2. Employment

In contrast to public spending, it is harder to get a sense of the number of workers in non-care services, especially as the same worker might provide a range of different services in the household. Nevertheless, it is possible to get an idea of workers associated with the specific household service policy instruments that may cover non-care, care and/or renovation work (the policies effects on employment over time are discussed in Section 4.7). In France, for example, the breadth of household service policies has led to a sizeable sector. For 2018, DARES (2020[71]) reported that about 1.3 million workers provided approximately 850 million hours of service work, two-thirds of which were in direct employment. Likewise, official German statistics do not differentiate between different care and non-care service types. Overall there were about 50 000 employees in service provider organisations in 2018, along with 304 000 marginal employees directly employed in households and 20 000 micro-entrepreneurs in 2016 (Ad-PHS, 2020[90]).

In Belgium and Sweden, all or almost all work is provided in the non-care sector. According to the Belgian National Social Security Office, there were about 150 000 providers employed as non-care household service workers in the fourth quarter of 2019, providing about 128 million hours of work in Belgium (IDEA Consult, 2018[100]; ONSS/RSZ, 2020[101]). Despite only small in differences in population size to Belgium, the Swedish RUT-sector only employed 21 868 workers that provided 22.9 million hours of services in the sector in 2019 (Skatteverket, 2021[102]).

The most recent employment figures for Finland indicate that about 4 900 service workers were providing approximately 10 000 hours of service work in 2012, which indicate particularly small employment levels (Ad-PHS, 2020[84]). However, this is substantially smaller than estimations based on domestic cleaners and helpers in the Finish Labour Force Survey (approx. 20 000, see Figure 2.1) and employment levels in private provider organisations, who predominately offer non-care service work and employed about 30 000 workers in 2013 (European Commission, 2015[103]).

4.5. Work arrangements and working conditions

4.5.1. Tripartite set-ups

The tripartite model is the most common work arrangement in many countries. This model includes third parties, usually service provider organisations, which mediate the non-care service provision in households. The service provider organisations can take a variety of forms, for example, for-profit businesses or non-profit associations, but public authorities can also provide services. In each of these settings, households purchase the services from the provider organisations, who then send their employees to provide services in the consumers' homes (Baga et al., 2020[3]).

Both the Swedish and the Belgian non-care household service policy frameworks are embedded in a tripartite system that generally does not allow for significant subsidies for direct domestic employment.[9] As such, only services bought through provider organisations are generally eligible for tax credits or social vouchers. In Sweden, these providers need to be registered as paying corporate tax and are usually for-profit, half of which are micro-entrepreneurs (Ad-PHS, 2020[82]). In Belgium, both for- and non-profit service providers are active in the market, along with some micro-entrepreneurs (Ad-PHS, 2020[87]). In Finland, 90% of household services are provided through intermediaries, both for- and non-profit. While both private and public agencies provide household services, it is predominately private providers that operate in the non-care sector (Ad-PHS, 2020[84]).

In general, **tripartite arrangements are linked to relatively good working conditions**. In countries where tripartite systems are the norm, wages are typically set by collective agreements (wages for other countries, where bipartite employment is more common, are discussed in the sub-section below). For Sweden, these specify a minimum salary of SEK 21 347 (PPP 2 405) per month at 40 hours per week in

2019, while receiving the same access to social security and employment protection as any other employee the country (Bowman and Cole, 2014[104]). The few workers not covered under collective agreements directly negotiate wages with their employers. Domestic cleaners in Finland earn a minimum of EUR 1 790 (PPP 2 121) per month at 37.5 hours per week in 2019 (Eurofound, 2020[105]; Ad-PHS, 2020[84]; Ad-PHS, 2020[82]). For all workers in the Belgian social voucher system, wages are set by collective agreement determined in a sectoral-level "*Joint Committee*" between worker and employer representatives. About 90% of these workers are registered under *Joint Committee 322.01 for accredited social voucher agencies*, which fixed gross wages at EUR 11.35 (PPP 15.05) to EUR 12.06 (PPP 15.99) per hour in 2020 (depending on seniority in the sector). This is substantially larger than the minimum wage of EUR 9.65 (PPP 12.73), and the small share of workers covered by other collective agreements can receive somewhat higher wages. For all workers, full social security rights are guaranteed and more than two-thirds of all contracts are indefinite, additionally guaranteeing at least 10 hours of work per week. The organisations that operate on the service voucher market are at all times requires to guarantee their employees well-being at work. As a result, the Belgian service voucher sector can be considered as "[...] the most regulated and protected [...]" domestic service sector in the world (European Commission, 2018[7]; Jokela, 2017[58]; Ramos Martin, 2020[106]; Lens et al., 2021[107]).

As such, working conditions in the sector are comparatively favourable, even though there are risks of exploitation for vulnerable workers, especially migrants (Ollus, 2016[108]; Michielsen, 2018[109]). In addition, substantial increases in numbers of employees on sick leave highlight increased workloads over the years and the relative arduousness of the tasks (Ramos Martin, 2020[106]). In Belgium, for example, entering the service voucher system increases the likelihood of claiming disability benefits in the short and long term (Leduc and Tojerow, 2020[110]). Even if sufficient health and safety regulations are present, there is also a general lack in monitoring and enforcement of existing regulations regarding occupational health and safety (Mousaid et al., 2017[111]; van Gerven, 2020[112]).

The household service policy instruments in France and Germany operate in mixed systems, where both bipartite and tripartite work arrangements eligible for tax credits or social vouchers and exist side by side. In Germany, households directly employ about 81% of workers as marginal employees under the *Minijob*-scheme, while about 19% work in for- and non-profit tripartite arrangements (Ad-PHS, 2020[90]). In France, about half of the households employ service workers directly, while the other half buy services from for- and non-profit provider organisations or other intermediaries in a tripartite system. The latter can take various forms, such as associations, businesses, or public organisations. There are two different models among them, the *mode prestataire*, which represents normal tripartite providers, or *mode mandataire*, where an organisation handles the administrative tasks of hiring domestic workers for private households while not employing service workers themselves (Ad-PHS, 2020[67]).[10] Overall, care work is predominantly provided by non-profit and public organisations, while for-profit organisation most often provide household service work (European Commission, 2018[7]).

Direct employment by households and its drawbacks

The bipartite model, also referred to as direct domestic employment, is another common formal work arrangement in which households hire service workers without an intermediary. In this case, the household acts as the legal employer and is therefore generally responsible for employer contributions (if the workers are covered). This work arrangement has been the most common model in numerous countries for many years. While still prominent in some countries, it has often been (partially) replaced by tripartite arrangements (Baga et al., 2020[3]).

The **wages in bipartite employment are comparatively low**. For example, directly employed French workers in the non-care household service sector earn on average about EUR 10 (PPP 11.84) net in 2012 (DARES, 2015[113]). Most of the German household service workers are entitled to the federal minimum wage of EUR 9.35 (PPP 12.60) per hour in 2020.[11] In addition, there is a range of different collective agreements that apply in specific regional contexts or service categories (Jaehrling and Weinkopf, 2020[114]).

More so than on the tripartite side of the market, **bipartite workers remain vulnerable in terms of job security and legal protection**. This differs somewhat from bipartite employment relationships in other sectors. For example, for outsourced business support services, workers in tripartite arrangements are usually paid less than directly employed workers and may be subject to worse health, safety and labour standards compliance by their employers (see OECD (2021[115])). In the context of household services however, many countries exclude domestic workers employed by households from health and safety regulations typically offered to other groups of workers. While this is grounded in difficulties in the application of the regulations in the domestic context, it often leaves household service workers unprotected and exposed to occupational hazards (Martin Ramos and Ruiz, 2020[4]).

In France, for example, labour inspectors need to obtain the occupants permission before entering the household, which is a strong limiting factor in terms of guaranteeing safety and quality (Ledoux and Krupka, 2020[116]).[12] In Germany, the *Minijob*-scheme exempts marginal workers from health- and unemployment insurance. At the same time, contributions towards pension insurance are relatively costly for employees in private households and often avoided due to the possibility of opting out (Jaehrling and Weinkopf, 2020[114]).

Related concerns apply in the United States, where many labour protections available to other groups of workers do not apply to domestic workers in bipartite work arrangements, such as the Occupational Safety and Health Act (Wolfe et al., 2020[117]). Even when workers are covered by state-level labour regulations, there can be substantial enforcement barriers based on fears around immigration-based retaliation, as more than half of all non-care household service workers are, often undocumented, non-citizen immigrants (Wolfe et al., 2020[117]; Theodore, Gutelius and Burnham, 2019[118]). In addition, only a small number of domestic workers are covered by social insurance. In addition, only 7% of housecleaners receive employer-provided health insurance coverage and only 2% have employer-provided retirement plans (Wolfe et al., 2020[117]).

Direct employment is also **linked to worse job quality**. For example, even though most bipartite work contracts in France are of a permanent nature, employing households can nevertheless terminate them easily. Overall, Devetter and Lefebvre (2015[119]) note that high degrees of part-time work, frequently changing private employers, limited employment protection, and relatively low net wages make bipartite household services in France a precarious sector.[13] However, while the French Labour Code explicitly excludes bipartite workers from many of its general provisions, most labour protections are provided through the Collective Agreement for Private Domestic Employees (Ledoux and Krupka, 2020[116]).[14]

Just as with in terms of working conditions, **bipartite work arrangements** may also **entail worse service quality** than in tripartite providers. As such, buying services from provider organisations ensures continuity of the service provision. For example, provider organisations can, for example, in case of illness send another worker, which is not necessarily possible for bipartite workers. Household purchasing services also avoid necessary administration tasks when employing a service worker (Ramos Martin and Ruiz, 2020[13]). Given that many countries have expanded the services eligible for tax credits and social vouchers over the years, tripartite systems may also be able to better react to this by diversifying their offered service portfolio, as they can easily hire new workers.

Other work arrangements

While bi- and tripartite work arrangements can be clearly classified, other arrangements fall somewhere between these two categories. For example, service workers may also register as self-employed micro-entrepreneurs. In this case, the service provider organisation consists of a single service worker, who, in contrast to the bipartite employment, benefits from the same regulations as for service providers. Similarly, micro-entrepreneurs sell services on the market, rather than being legally employed by the household. However, in terms of labour and social protection, the service provision through self-employment can resemble domestic employment. As such, this employment model shares aspects of both direct employment and service provider arrangements (Baga et al., 2020[3]; European Commission, 2015[12]).

In France, some businesses are micro-enterprises, though they provide just about 1% of all hours worked in the sector (Ad-PHS, 2020[67]). In Germany, about 40% of tripartite employees are in fact self-employed, which excludes them from minimum wage entitlements. In addition, online service platforms have become an important player on the German household service market in recent years (Ad-PHS, 2020[90]). As laid out in Section 2.3, the exact employment form in this arrangements if often unclear, which can undermine job quality and labour protections for these workers.

Against the backdrop of widespread precarious conditions in the household service market – predominately for bipartite arrangements, but also for workers in provider organisations – the *ILO Convention 189 on Domestic Work* from 2011 stipulates a set of minimum rights for domestic workers (see Box 4.6). To this date, the convention has been ratified by 32 countries, including a number of OECD countries, prompting new and strengthened employment protection and social security provision. When Finland ratified the convention in 2015, household service workers were granted the same labour rights as other workers in the country. As such, regular working time was limited to 8 hours, in contrast to earlier legislations prescribing 9 hours as a standard. Workers were also covered by social security, much like the rest of the country (van Gerven, 2020[112]). In other cases, for example in Belgium, most of the prescribed labour protections were already present in the national legal framework for domestic work before ratification in 2015 (European Commission, 2018[7]; Ramos Martin, 2020[106]).[15] However, even if ILO Convention 189 is ratified, some countries still have considerable gaps in the implementation and enforcement of guarantees as stipulated under the Convention, both regarding informal and formal workers (ILO, 2021[120]). For example, despite the general guarantee of equal treatment for marginal employees in Germany, deviations from these stipulations are widespread in practice (e.g. in terms of sick pay and paid holidays) (Jaehrling and Weinkopf, 2020[114]).

Box 4.6. ILO Convention 189 on Domestic Work

The *ILO Convention 189 on Domestic Work* was signed in 2011 with a strong majority in favour among delegates, after a 2-year negotiation with substantial involvement of a broad coalition of workers themselves. The convention aims at ensuring decent work conditions for domestic workers and requires ratifying member countries to implement a range of legal protections. Among others, it stipulates the following guarantees:

- Protection from abuse, harassment, and violence (*Article 5*)
- Fair terms of employment and working conditions (*Article 6*)
- Sufficient information on employment terms (*Article 7*)
- Protections for migrant workers (*Article 8*)
- Equal treatment in terms of employment conditions (*Article 10*)
- Minimum wage entitlement, where applicable (*Article 11*)
- Safe and healthy working environments (*Article 13*)
- Equal treatment in terms of social security protection (*Article 14*)
- Labour inspections and penalties (*Article 17*).

The convention thus postulates that all domestic workers are entitled to protective labour legislations and social security provisions. As of today, it has been ratified by 32 ILO member countries and therefore demands often significant improvement in working conditions for domestic employees.*

Note: Of the countries primarily discussed in this report, only France did not ratify ILO convention 189 yet.
Source: ILO Domestic Workers Convention – C189, Pape (2016[121]), ILO (2021[120]).

4.6. Professionalization and training

A critical aspect in ensuring high service quality and professionalization in the household service sector is the enforcement of qualification standards and provision of training. In most of the considered countries, there is no direct qualification enforcement for the non-care household service sector, however. As such, service quality regulations are much looser than in the care sector, which is often rather strict in qualification requirements. The only exception is Belgium, where service vouchers are limited to licensed service provider companies. While there are no strict qualification requirements for workers themselves, regional and sectoral training funds provide regular training. As such, 12 hours of training per year are compulsory for workers under the service voucher scheme. Training is subject to financial incentives and provider organisations can receive partial reimbursement on the training costs as well as extra subsidies from regional training funds for new workers coming out of unemployment or integration benefits. In addition, the sectoral training funds finance up to 18 hours of training for new workers employed under collective agreement 322.01 for accredited service voucher agencies (Ramos Martin, 2020[106]; Ad-PHS, 2020[87]).

Other countries provide voluntary certification or qualification systems for service workers and provider organisations. For example, a voluntary, yet not well recognised, quality charters for intermediary organisations exist in the Swedish RUT sector. Workers themselves can get certified by the Service Industry Professional Board (*Servicebranschens Yrkesnämnd*) after completing theoretical, oral and practical tests on cleaning and household services (Ad-PHS, 2020[82]).[16] In Finland, the government established a 3-year basic vocational qualification in Household and Cleaning Services in 2000 to improve professionalism in the sector, which was integrated with the Cleaning Service Qualification in 2010 (European Commission, 2015[103]).

It is also **tripartite arrangements** that **offer better opportunities for training and upskilling** of the service workers. In Sweden, many provider companies, especially larger ones, have their own training system that ensures quality provision of household services (Ad-PHS, 2020[82]). In addition, French service workers in provider organisations more often benefit from training through their employers (Devetter and Lefebvre, 2015[119]). In Germany, a conceptual qualification framework for new employees of service provider organisation has been developed by the German Society for Housekeeping. Within this framework, new workers can receive up to 12 weeks of structured training aimed at equipping them with the necessary skills for the job (Ad-PHS, 2020[90]; Jaehrling and Weinkopf, 2020[114]).

Resulting from widespread employment in **bipartite arrangements**, most of the directly employed household service workers in Germany and France have **little or no professional training** in domestic work however. In these arrangements, sufficient qualifications and standards can become secondary to price levels, which can negatively affect the professionalization of the providers. However, there are some mechanisms in place that aim to improve quality in the sector. For example, through collective agreements in France, private employers pay a direct contribution to the vocational training of their employees, who can thus access trainings in order to improve service quality. In the absence of formal qualifications, workers with a minimum of one year full-time work experience can have their skills recognised through a vocational certification (*Validation des acquis de l'expérience*), conditional on passing general and professional tests (Devetter and Lefebvre, 2015[119]; Baga et al., 2020[3]; European Commission, 2018[7]; Ad-PHS, 2020[90]; Jaehrling and Weinkopf, 2020[114]).

4.7. Effects of the policies

4.7.1. Consumption patterns

Non-care household service policies have undoubtedly created financial incentives to use declared over undeclared services. As such, the overall formal household service sector has generally seen growth in terms of consumption (see Figure 4.2). For example, for the Belgian service voucher, which is the most widely used incentive scheme considered in this report, the number of consumers steadily increased from 4% at its inception to about 23% of all Belgians by the end of 2016. This overall success may be due to a comparatively high elasticity of demand with respect to the price of household services (Desiere and Goesaert, 2019[122]).

Both Finland and Sweden have also seen increased household service consumption over the years, even though both differ in terms of how much of this can be attributed to the tax credits. With slow, but almost steady growth in recipients, the Finish DHSTC reached about 17% of households in 2019. Only when the generosity of the tax credit was reduced between 2011 and 2012 did consumption drop about 2 percentage points. Despite these trends, the growth in the number of households using the tax credits was weaker compared to neighbouring Sweden, where most users state they would not consume household services if it were not for the price reduction of the tax credit (Ad-PHS, 2020[82]). The RUT-sector itself has seen stronger growth over the years, reaching 19% of Swedish households in 2019. This may therefore reveal a larger demand elasticity with respect to the net price of the services than in Finland (Harju et al., 2021[83]).

Figure 4.2. Consumption patterns

Share of private households consuming household services with specific policy incentives, all eligible services

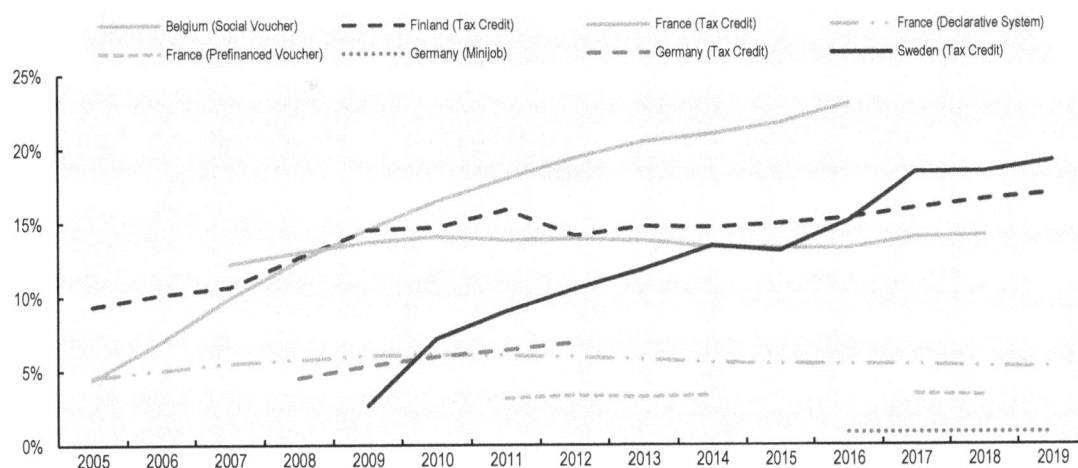

Note: The presented data divides the total reported data by the total number of private households as reported by Eurostat. Therefore, the share of actual household consumers might be different. For example, some households may have two or more members consuming tax credit or vouchers. Data for all countries, except for Belgium, also contains care related services, as well as renovation work for Finland. For Germany, the tax credit data concerns only household service work and not renovation services. The minijob data concerns only marginal employment in private households. For France, the tax credit data concerns tax filings for the deduction, but it is not necessarily the case that each claimant was granted a credit. For 2016 and 2017, there is no public data on the number of households receiving prefinanced CESU vouchers.
Source: OECD calculations based on Eurostat Household Data and Skatteverket (Sweden), Bundesrechnungshof (Germany), Minijob-Zentrale (Germany), IDEA Consult (Belgium), Suomen virallinen tilasto (Finland), Verohallinto (Finland), Direction Générale des Finances Publique (France), ACOSS (France), Direction Générale des Entreprises (France), Association Professionnelle des Emetteurs de CESU (France).

With the exception of two amendments of the tax code to allow for refundability, the French household service tax credit has not been subject to major changes. As such, its consumption has remained largely stable at around 14% of all French households. Both CESU instruments (declarative and pre-financed) have been equally stable, but used by no more than 5% of all households.

There is limited public data on the number of households consuming the German tax credits over the years. However, the Federal Audit Office shows that the number of households receiving tax credits for household services increased by roughly 50% between 2008 and 2012 (excluding renovation services). About a third of these households would have used formal household services even in the absence of the tax credit (Bundesrechnungshof, 2016[123]). The share of private households hiring marginal employees for household service work has been about 0.8% between 2016 and 2019.

4.7.2. Consumption groups

Most household service policy frameworks aim – at least to some degree – to ease the housework burden for families, especially those with two earners and/or young dependent children. Given that these households are in most cases also earn more than an average household, one might expect that the fiscal incentives are more likely to reach better-off households. These patterns have been criticised by a number of researchers as there are concerns that the current systems predominately cater to high-income earners, effectively subsidising their leisure time (e.g. Nyberg (2015[124]) or Carbonnier (2015[72])). At the same time, one must note that there is an overall lack of criticism for tax subsidies that target work traditionally associated to men, such as tax credits for renovation work (e.g. the ROT-deduction in Sweden, which has comparable consumption patterns to the RUT-deduction). That the criticism is geared toward female-dominated work may reveal the general undervaluation of these tasks relative to male-dominated work.

It is indeed in the nature of tax credits that more often households of higher incomes claim tax credits and their deduction volume is in most cases larger than at lower incomes (Figure 4.3). For example, more than one-third of the highest earners benefits from the RUT-deduction in Sweden, while also receiving service work of the highest volume (Figure 4.3, Panel A.). At the same time, a significant number of customers with medium-low incomes benefit from the tax reliefs that are of only slightly lower volume than credits for moderate income earners. In Finland, the average credit volumes are relatively stable and similar across the income distribution, while there is a much stronger gradient across income groups in terms of usage (Figure 4.3, Panel B.). Many of the households with lower incomes may receive social vouchers or care allowances that disqualify households from the tax credit, but they might also not be able to claim tax credits due to insufficient levels of taxable income. The higher consumption among lower-income households in Sweden may therefore be a result of granting the tax credit at source, which relieves households from paying the full service price upfront.

While there is no unified national data on consumption across income groups for the German tax credits and Belgian service vouchers, regional data, for example on Flanders (Belgium) and Rhineland-Palatinate (Germany), show similar patterns of predominant consumption by better earning households (Vlaamse DWSE, 2020[94]; Statistisches Landesamt Rheinland-Pfalz, 2018[125]). In Flanders, these numbers mirror earlier findings that highlighted the inability to reach a substantial share of less-affluent households and predominately cater to two-earner household in full-time work (Marx and Vandelannoote, 2015[62]). For France, there is no data that breaks down consumption by income groups since the generalisation of refundability (for earlier data see DARES (2014[126])).

In terms of other household characteristics, those of retirement age are also more likely to use household services. In Sweden, for example, the retired were the biggest population group using the RUT deduction, reaching 20% of those above the age of 75 in 2018. Among all age groups, it is women who make the most use of the RUT deduction, especially between ages 35 and 59 (Skatteverket, 2020[127]; Ekonomifakta, 2020[128]). For Finland, Aalto (2015[60]) shows that those with particular need for household help, namely families with children and the elderly, make higher use of the DHSTC than the average household.

Figure 4.3. Tax credit consumption by income group

A. Sweden: Share of population receiving and average volume of RUT by taxable income, 2018

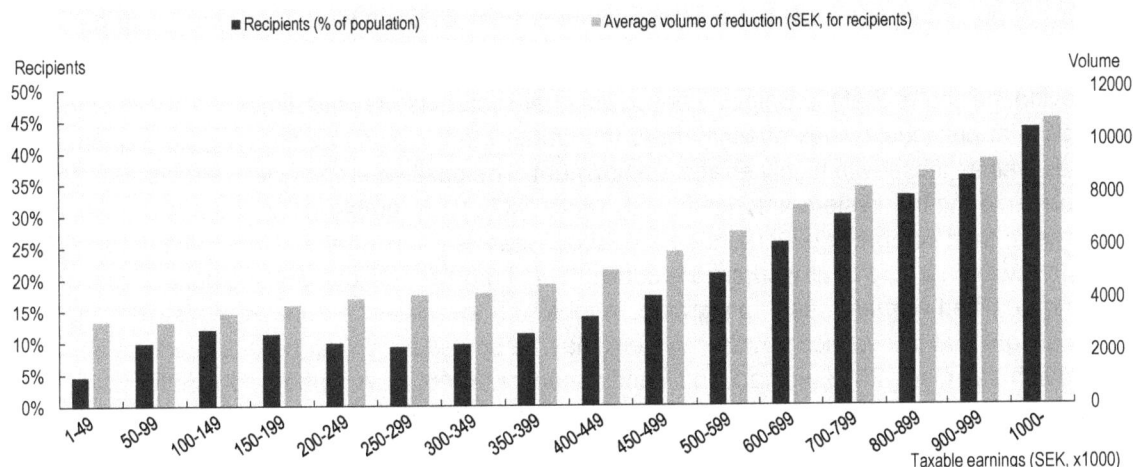

B. Finland: Share receiving and average volume of DHSTC by taxable income, 2019

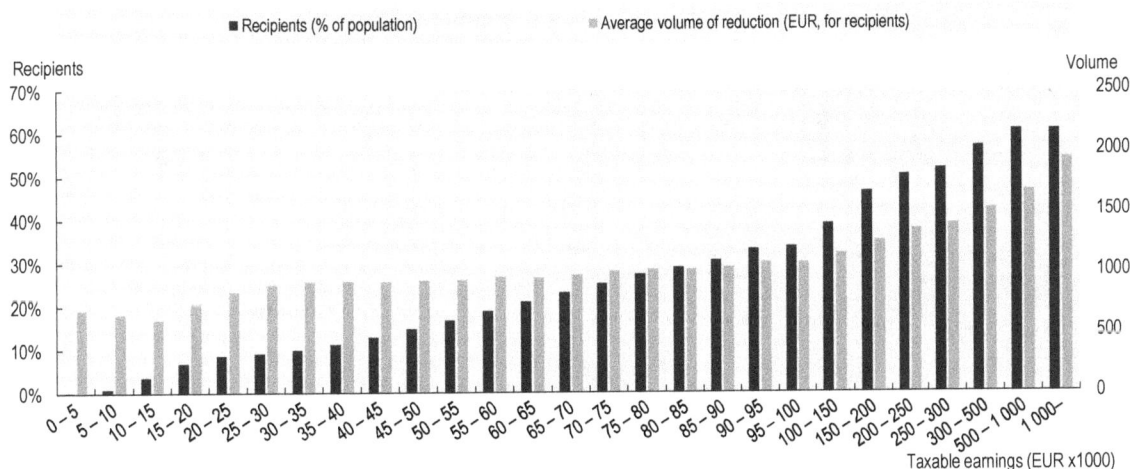

Source: Statistiska Centralbyrån (2020[129]), Verohallinto (2021[98]).

4.7.3. Household service employment

With increasing users, household service policy instruments have also led to sizeable employment in the sector (Figure 4.4). These employees might come from both previously declared and undeclared positions, or from entirely other sectors following increased attractively of household service employment (see e.g. Marx and Vandelannoote (2015[62])). However, the growth in the number of employees differs strongly across countries, which can be linked to differences in scope and, particularly, the generosity of the policies.

The French household service policies have, in some shape or form, been in place for about three decades. As such, employment in the overall sector has not seen major increases over recent years. In fact, by 2018 it fell to approximately 4.9% of all employment, down from 5.7% in 2010. This decrease is predominately due to a reduction of workers in bipartite arrangements, while employment in provider organisations is slowly but continuously increasing (DARES, 2020[71]). In contrast, employment in the Belgian service voucher sector increased (almost) steadily, despite only applying to no n-care services. These are making up 3.1% of the Belgian labour force in 2019, many of which work part-time while caring for their own household (ONSS/RSZ, 2020[101]). However, the dynamics of employment in the Belgian sector may not be perfectly comparable over time, as measurement has changed, for example by integrating those employed by provincial and local government services from 2017 onward. More complete data may be found in (Lens et al., 2021[107]).

Recent evidence shows that the Belgian service voucher system is drawing almost half of its workers from individuals with previously weak attachment to the labour market, such as the long-term unemployed or inactive as well as those with highly erratic employment. The positive employment effects are permanent, as workers entering the system are significantly more likely to be employed in the sector over the short and long term than comparable workers on the labour market (Lens et al., 2021[107]; Leduc and Tojerow, 2020[110]). However, a third of all workers are coming out of regular employment in other sectors, potentially entrapping qualified women, often immigrants, in jobs with low career prospects. As such, these hidden effects highlight that the service voucher system may be somewhat too generous (Lens et al., 2021[107]; Raz-Yurovich and Marx, 2018[63]; Marx and Vandelannoote, 2015[62]). A further problem for lower-qualified Belgians in finding employment is that labour migration may have crowded them out of the sector. Especially in Brussels, more than three-quarters of all service voucher workers are foreigners, many of which are coming from Eastern Europe (Marx and Vandelannoote, 2015[62]; IDEA Consult, 2020[95]).

Figure 4.4. Employment related to household service policy instruments

Share of employees associated with specific household service policy instruments among total employed work force

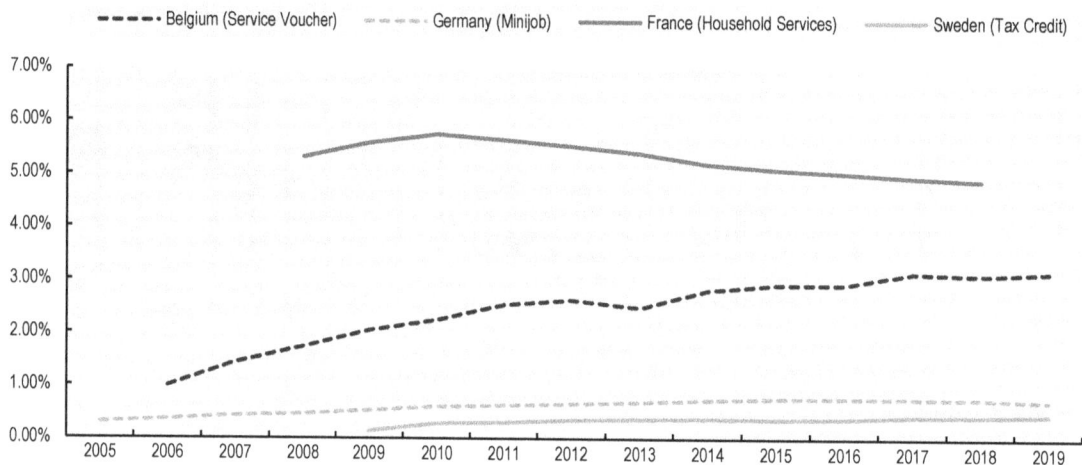

Note: These figures here generally report employment related to one or more of the household service policy instruments. They thus differ from data reported through Labour Force Surveys, as displayed in Figure 2.1. As explained above, the latter are no perfect measure of employment in the overall sector and only include domestic cleaners and helpers. Data for Belgium refers to workers associated with the service voucher sector in the fourth quarter of each year. Data collection methods have changed after 2013 and 2017, thus the data may not be fully comparable over time. Data for Germany only concern only marginal employment in private households, which can be either care or non-care work. Data for France contain all household service employment, which covers both care and non-care work. This might be financed by tax credits, CESU vouchers as well as VAT or employer contribution exemptions. The data for Sweden only concern work in the RUT sector, which covers both care and non-care work. There is no sufficient data for Finland.
Source: OECD calculations based on Skatteverket (2021[102]), ONSS/RSZ (2020[101]; 2016[130]), DARES (2020[71]), Minijob-Zentrale (2020[131]), Enste (2017[132]).

Employment in the Swedish RUT-sector is on a substantially lower level, despite continuous positive trends. Over the last 10 years, employment in the sector has almost doubled, reaching 0.4% of the Swedish labour force in 2020. In total, estimates suggest that the RUT-deduction has directly led to the creation of at least 8 500 jobs, almost half of all employment in the RUT-sector (Tillväxtanalys, 2019[133]). While a primary motivation of the tax credit was to integrate female refugees into the Swedish labour market, recent evidence highlights that the majority of the foreign-born workers in the sector are temporary labour migrants from other European countries (Rickne, 2019[64]).

Unfortunately, it is only possible to measure the development of marginal employment in private households over time for Germany. Despite remaining relatively low, marginal employment roughly doubled since 2005, reaching 0.7% of the labour force in 2019 (Minijob-Zentrale, 2020[131]; Enste, 2017[132]).[17] Likewise, it is complicated to obtain clear statistics on the number of Finnish household service employees over time. However, Harju et al. (2021[83]) suggests that the tax credit likely did not substantially increase employment in the Finish household service sector, much in line with similar evidence for VAT-reduction experiments in other labour-intensive service sectors (see e.g. Benzarti et al. (2020[134]) and Kosonen (2015[135])).

4.7.4. Undeclared work

With the before-mentioned financial incentives for formal household service consumption, the incentives to consume undeclared services are likewise reduced. As such, there have been noticeable effects on the undeclared household service sector across the selected countries.

For example, a survey-based study of the Swedish Tax Authority shows the share of households consuming undeclared household services decreased from 6% in 2005 to 1% in 2019. As a result, RUT and the related ROT-reduction led to an approximate decrease in the consumption of undeclared services from SEK 11 billion (PPP 1.16 billion) to SEK 3 billion (PPP 0.34 billion) over the same time (Skatteverket, 2020[127]). Likewise, the French household service policies had a substantial effect on undeclared work in the sector as well. While half of all household service work was provided informally in 1996, it fell to 20% by 2015 (CRÉDOC, 2017[15]; DARES, 2014[126]).[18] The reduction in undeclared employment in the sector was particularly strong over the first 10 years the initial *Chèque Emploi Service* and *Titre Emploi-Service* systems were active, but was further enhanced with introduction of the CESU (DARES, 2014[126]).

The effects of household service policies on the incidence of undeclared work is related to its capacity to set a competitive price on the formal market. In Sweden where substantial tax credits prevail, "after tax credit" prices of non-household services are relatively competitive and have led to sizeable reductions in informality. In contrast, undeclared household service work is widespread in Germany where the tax credits are relatively low and and have limited impact of the price of the services. As such, about 89% of all household service jobs in Germany were provided in an informal setting in 2017. This is only slightly lower than 94% in 2005, shortly after the introduction of tax credits and marginal employment schemes (Enste, 2019[8]). As a result, the Federal Audit Office strongly doubts the effectiveness of the existing German household service policy framework in reducing undeclared employment (Bundesrechnungshof, 2016[123]).

Despite previously estimating a reduction of undeclared work in the sector from 60% to 25% by 2010, the Finnish Ministries of Employment and Economy see methodological problems in measuring the deadweight effect of the schemes. Therefore there have been no recent evaluations of the DHSTC, especially regarding the extent of undeclared work in the sector (European Commission, 2015[103]). As the only recent study on these effects, Harju et al. (2021[83]) use the introduction of comparable household service tax credits at different times in Finland and Sweden, two countries with relatively similar economic development and demographics. The findings suggest that the tax credit likely had very little impact on decreasing the incidence of undeclared work and tax evasion.

In some instances, the reduction in the relative share of undeclared work may also be linked disproportionate increases in new consumers of declared services, rather than actual reductions in informal service provision. For example, survey data for Belgium suggests only a modest shift from undeclared to declared work (Marx and Vandelannoote, 2015[62]). Therefore, most of the current users of declared services are new consumers rather than previous users of undeclared services, as evident in Flemish survey data (Vlaamse DWSE, 2020[94]).

4.7.5. Female employment

A main motivation for household service polices is to relieve households from the burden of unpaid housework. Given that women predominantly bear this burden (see page 19) and the majority of the opportunities for economic value creation lies with them, most of these effects are to be expected among them.

There is some evidence on policy effects on increased female labour force participation. For example, Halldén and Stenberg (2018[136]) found that 40-70 hours of RUT-deducted household service work per year proportionally increase the income and employment of married women in Sweden, who use 60% of their freed time in the labour market. In addition, positive employment and income effects of the tax credits seem to be concentrated among dual earner families with children, rather than for single parents and people above retirement age (Riksrevisionen, 2020[91]). For Belgium, the service voucher system appears to have had positive short- and long-term effects on women's employment for both high- and low-skilled women as well as female unemployed (Desiere and Goesaert, 2019[122]; Raz-Yurovich and Marx, 2018[63]). However, estimations of employment effects of the social voucher scheme are not straightforward and and because of insufficient data have to rely on assumptions.

Evaluations on the effect of the French household service policies on female labour supply are rare. However, women in households that used domestic services were 9.4 percentage points more likely to be in employment than in the average household in 2005, increasing further with the number of dependent children in the household. While this may be tainted by reverse causation, it nevertheless exhibits a clear link between employment and household service consumption (Marbot, 2009[137]). At the same time, the consumption of household services gradually increases with educational qualification and the number of hours worked (Devetter, 2017[138]). This suggests that household services are an important substitute for unpaid housework in families were both adults engage in full-time and career-oriented work.

In both Finland and Germany, there is a lack of evaluations on household service policies and the labour force participation of women. However, about one-third of German household service consumers report that they do so in order to have more time to engage on the labour market. At the same time, 22% of those without domestic help report that they would like to do so in order to increase their engagement on the labour market (Juncke, Krämer and Weinelt, 2019[92]).

4.7.6. Earn-back effects

At face value, household service policies can appear as expensive fiscal measures. However, a naïve focus on the cost of these instruments curtails potential earn-back effects that may substantially lower the net costs and, in some cases, could even lead to net fiscal benefits. These earn-back effects are of a direct or indirect nature. Reduced expenditure on unemployment benefits and increased income tax revenues and social contributions are directly earned back. Indirect effects relate to increased business activity as well as consumption and labour market substitution effects. Against this backdrop, it is important to account for such earn-back effects, even though their estimation is complicated and usually based on a number assumptions (EFSI, 2013[139]). While presenting the overall costs for household service policies, if possible narrowed down to non-care services in isolation, this sub-section thus also provides figures on earn-back effects wherever possible.

In practice, estimates often point toward budget neutrality of household service policies, such as in France and Belgium. In the French non-care household service sector, the earn-back effects were estimated to be EUR 70 million (PPP 87 million) larger than the public expenses in the sector in 2014 (Lebrun and Fourna, 2016[93]). After accounting for direct and indirect earn-back effects, the net cost of the Belgian social voucher in 2016 were estimated at EUR 1 200 (PPP 1 536) per full-job and thus remarkably small compared to the overall size of the policy intervention (IDEA Consult, 2018[100]).[19] However, these calculations assume a particularly small role of deadweight, substitution and displacement effects of the social vouchers, leading to high estimated net job creation (e.g. 90% in Flanders, see IDEA Consult (2019[140])).[20] This, in turn, results in an estimation of stark reductions in expenditure on unemployment benefits. In light of the strong labour migration into the service voucher system, particularly in Brussels, as well as the entry of many workers from non-subsidized jobs (see Section 4.7.3), these assumptions may prove to be too optimistic.

There is considerable doubt on whether the Swedish RUT-system is self-financing. Summing up direct and indirect earn-back effects, a deficit of approximately SEK 1.1 billion (PPP 0.12 billion), or 0.03% of GDP, remains. The real wedge between costs and earn-back effects may even be larger as this calculation excludes consumption effects. These can reduce the earn-back, as households shift their expenses toward household services and decrease revenue elsewhere (Riksrevisionen, 2020[91]). However, given that the Swedish household service policies appear to have reduced undeclared work and increased female labour force participation, despite missing the target of integrating refugees into the labour market, these moderate net costs may have been warranted.

There is no recent evaluation of earn-back effects of household service policies in Finland and Germany. However, given the limited effects mentioned above, Harju et al. (2021[83]) note that the costs of the Finish tax credits are likely higher than their benefits. Early estimates concluded a net benefit of almost EUR 150 million (PPP 154 million) for the overall tax credit in 2004 (Niilola and Valtakari, 2006[141]). A German pilot-project, was operational in 2 districts in the state of Baden-Württemberg between 2017 and 2019. The project introduced a social voucher for non-care household services, based on the Belgian system. The subsequent cost-benefit evaluation highlights potential earn-back effects, particularly in terms of tax revenue and social security contributions in the long term that are larger than the public expenditure on the social vouchers (Meier-Gräwe, 2019[142]). For potential increases in public subsidies, model simulations based on different scenarios on the overall German non-care household service market predict direct earn-back effects that are lower than the aggregated costs. However, increased returns through indirect effects may substantially increase the earn-back and make future implementations of substantial non-care household service policies viable in the mid to long term (Juncke, Krämer and Weinelt, 2019[92]).[21]

References

Aalto, K. (2015), "The Finnish Tax Reduction for Domestic Costs: Consumption Patterns", in *The Political Economy of Household Services in Europe*, Palgrave Macmillan UK, London, http://dx.doi.org/10.1057/9781137473721_11. [60]

Ad-PHS (2020), *Country Report: Austria*, https://ad-phs.eu/ht8ag2/uploads/2021/01/cr_-ad-phs-country-report-austria-may-2020-rev-2020-11-23.pdf. [143]

Ad-PHS (2020), *Country Report: Belgium*, https://ad-phs.eu/ht8ag2/uploads/2021/01/cr_belgium_.pdf. [87]

Ad-PHS (2020), *Country Report: Finland*, https://ad-phs.eu/ht8ag2/uploads/2020/12/ad-phs-country-report-finland-2020-.pdf. [84]

Ad-PHS (2020), *Country Report: France*, https://ad-phs.eu/ht8ag2/uploads/2021/01/cr_france_.pdf. [67]

Ad-PHS (2020), *Country Report: Germany*, https://ad-phs.eu/ht8ag2/uploads/2020/12/ad-phs-country-report-germany_december-2020.pdf. [90]

Ad-PHS (2020), *Country Report: Italy*, https://ad-phs.eu/ht8ag2/uploads/2021/05/country-report-italy-en.pdf. [149]

Ad-PHS (2020), *Country Report: Luxembourg*, https://ad-phs.eu/ht8ag2/uploads/2021/05/ad-phs-country-report-luxembourg_en-1.pdf. [151]

Ad-PHS (2020), *Country Report: Spain*, https://ad-phs.eu/ht8ag2/uploads/2021/05/ad-phs-_country-report_spain_en-1.pdf. [155]

Ad-PHS (2020), *Country Report: Sweden*, https://ad-phs.eu/ht8ag2/uploads/2019/11/ad-phs-country-report-sweden-eng.pdf. [82]

Ad-PHS (2020), *Country Report: The Netherlands*, https://ad-phs.eu/ht8ag2/uploads/2020/12/cr_netherlands.pdf. [153]

Ad-PHS (2020), *Social Voucher Programs: Tailored Guidance*, https://ad-phs.eu/ht8ag2/uploads/2021/05/03-social-voucher-programs-tailored-guidance_eng-1.pdf. [86]

Ad-PHS (2020), *Tailored Guidance for Digital Platforms and Networks*, https://ad-phs.eu/ht8ag2/uploads/2020/12/01-tailored-guidance-for-digital-platforms-networks_eng.pdf. [20]

Ad-PHS (2020), *The Short-Term Impact of COVID-19 on the Field of PHS*, https://ad- [23]

phs.eu/ht8ag2/uploads/2020/12/ad-phs-covid_report_december-2020_final_editing.pdf.

Ahmad, N. and S. Koh (2011), "Incorporating Estimates of Household Production of Non-Market Services into International Comparisons of Material Well-Being", *OECD Statistics Working Papers*, No. 2011/7, OECD Publishing, Paris, https://dx.doi.org/10.1787/5kg3h0jgk87g-en. [53]

Alon, T. et al. (2020), *The Impact of COVID-19 on Gender Equality The Impact of COVID-19 on Gender Equality **, http://www.crctr224.de (accessed on 25 January 2021). [50]

Angermann, A. and W. Eichhorst (2013), "Who cares for you at home? Personal and household services in Europe", *IZA Policy Paper, No. 71*, http://hdl.handle.net/10419/91809. [157]

Ashok, V. and G. Huber (2020), "Do Means of Program Delivery and Distributional Consequences Affect Policy Support? Experimental Evidence About the Sources of Citizens' Policy Opinions", *Political Behavior*, Vol. 42, pp. 1097–1118, http://dx.doi.org/10.1007/s11109-019-09534-z. [66]

Baga, E. et al. (2020), *Personal and Household Services (PHS) Policies and Instruments: State of Play in the 21 EU Member States*, https://ad-phs.eu/ht8ag2/uploads/2020/12/state-of-play-report_december-2020.pdf. [3]

Benzarti, Y. et al. (2020), "What Goes Up May Not Come Down: Asymmetric Incidence of Value-Added Taxes", *Journal of Political Economy*, Vol. 128/12, pp. 4438-4474, http://dx.doi.org/10.1086/710558. [134]

Bertelsmann Stiftung (2020), *Rollen und Aufgabenverteilung bei Frauen und Männern in Corona-Zeiten: Ergebnisse einer repräsentativen Umfrage*, https://www.bertelsmann-stiftung.de/de/publikationen/publikation/did/rollen-und-aufgabenverteilung-bei-frauen-und-maennern-in-corona-zeiten. [48]

Bhargava, S. and D. Manoli (2015), "Psychological Frictions and the Incomplete Take-Up of Social Benefits: Evidence from an IRS Field Experiment", *American Economic Review*, Vol. 105/11, pp. 3489-3529, http://dx.doi.org/10.1257/aer.20121493. [77]

Bianchi, S. et al. (2000), "Is Anyone Doing the Housework? Trends in the Gender Division of Household Labor", *Social Forces*, Vol. 79/1, pp. 191-228, http://dx.doi.org/10.1093/sf/79.1.191. [30]

Bianchi, S. et al. (2012), "Housework: Who Did, Does or Will Do It, and How Much Does It Matter?", *Social Forces*, Vol. 91/1, pp. 55-63, http://dx.doi.org/10.1093/sf/sos120. [31]

Boivin, L. (2017), "Chèque Service, Normes Du Travail Et Liberté D'association : Le Cas Du Québec", *LLDRL Working Paper Series*, Vol. 8, https://www.mcgill.ca/lldrl/files/lldrl/boivin_wp8_3.pdf. [89]

Bowman, J. and A. Cole (2014), "Cleaning the 'People's Home': The Politics of the Domestic Service Market in Sweden", *Gender, Work & Organization*, Vol. 21/2, pp. 187-201, http://dx.doi.org/10.1111/gwao.12029. [104]

Bundesminsterium der Finanzen (2019), *Bericht der Bundesregierung über die Entwicklung der Finanzhilfen des Bundes und der Steuervergünstigungen für die Jahre 2017 bis 2020 (27. Subventionsbericht)*, [99] https://www.bundesfinanzministerium.de/Content/DE/Downloads/Broschueren_Bestellservice/2020-03-01-Subventionsbericht.pdf?__blob=publicationFile&v=16.

Bundesrechnungshof (2016), *Steuerermäßigung für Handwerkerleistungen und haushaltsnahe Dienstleistungen nach § 35a Einkommensteuergesetz*, https://www.bundesrechnungshof.de/de/veroeffentlichungen/produkte/beratungsberichte/langfassungen/langfassungen-2016/2016-bericht-steuerermaessigung-fuer-handwerkerleistungen-und-haushaltsnahe-dienstleistungen-nach-35a-einkommensteuergesetz-pdf/at_downloa. [123]

Burnham, L. and N. Theodore (2012), *Home Economics: The Invisible and Unregulated World of Domestic Work*, https://www.domesticworkers.org/home-economics-invisible-and-unregulated-world-domestic-work. [18]

Carbonnier, C. (2015), "Job Creation, Public Cost and the Distributive Profile of Tax Allowances for Household Services in France", in *The Political Economy of Household Services in Europe*, Palgrave Macmillan UK, London, http://dx.doi.org/10.1057/9781137473721_12. [72]

Carlson, D., R. Petts and J. Pepin (2020), *Changes in Parents' Domestic Labor During the COVID-19 Pandemic*, Center for Open Science, http://dx.doi.org/10.31235/osf.io/jy8fn. [41]

Chetty, R., A. Looney and K. Kroft (2009), "Salience and Taxation: Theory and Evidence", *American Economic Review*, Vol. 99/4, pp. 1145-1177, http://dx.doi.org/10.1257/aer.99.4.1145. [81]

Chetty, R. and E. Saez (2013), "Teaching the Tax Code: Earnings Responses to an Experiment with EITC Recipients", *American Economic Journal: Applied Economics*, Vol. 5/1, pp. 1-31, http://dx.doi.org/10.1257/app.5.1.1. [78]

Cour des comptes de Belgique (2018), *Projets de décrets contenant le premier ajustement des budgets pour l'année 2018 de la Région wallonne*, https://www.ccrek.be/docs/2018_23_BudgetRW2018A1.pdf. [96]

CRÉDOC (2017), *Une première enquête pilote en France sur le travail dissimulé*, https://www.credoc.fr/publications/une-premiere-enquete-pilote-en-france-sur-le-travail-dissimule. [15]

DARES (2020), *Les services à la personne en 2018*, http://www.epsilon.insee.fr/jspui/bitstream/1/120406/1/2020-011.pdf. [71]

DARES (2020), *Résultats de l'enquête flash Covid-19 auprès des organismes de services à la personne*, https://dares.travail-emploi.gouv.fr/sites/default/files/pdf/dares_resultats_enquete_covid19_services-personne.pdf. [24]

DARES (2019), *Les dépenses en faveur de l'emploi et du marché du travail en 2017: Une forte hausse liée au crédit d'impôt pour la compétitivité et l'emploi*, http://www.epsilon.insee.fr/jspui/bitstream/1/108505/1/2019-047.pdf. [69]

DARES (2015), *Services à la personne: aides publiques et coût pour l'utilisateur*, https://dares.travail-emploi.gouv.fr/publications/services-a-la-personne-aides-publiques-et-cout-pour-l-utilisateur. [113]

DARES (2014), *Les services à la personne. Qui y recourt? Et à quel coût?*, https://www.servicesalapersonne.gouv.fr/files_sap/files/images-activites/dares-analyses-063.pdf. [126]

Del Boca, D. et al. (2020), "Women's and men's work, housework and childcare, before and during COVID-19", *Review of Economics of the Household*, Vol. 18/4, pp. 1001-1017, http://dx.doi.org/10.1007/s11150-020-09502-1. [39]

Desiere, S. and T. Goesaert (2019), "The employment effect of the Belgian service voucher system", *SPSW Working Paper*, Vol. CeSo/SPSW/2019-07. [122]

Devetter, F. (2017), "Changes in Demand for Paid Domestic Help", in *INED Population Studies, A Longitudinal Approach to Family Trajectories in France*, Springer International Publishing, Cham, http://dx.doi.org/10.1007/978-3-319-56001-4_11. [138]

Devetter, F. and M. Lefebvre (2015), "Employment Quality in the Sector of Personal and Household Services: Status and Impact of Public Policies in France", in *The Political Economy of Household Services in Europe*, Palgrave Macmillan UK, London, http://dx.doi.org/10.1057/9781137473721_7. [119]

DGCIS (2011), *Étude sur les services à la personne dans sept pays européens*, https://archives.entreprises.gouv.fr/2012/www.pme.gouv.fr/essentiel/etudesstat/pdf/services-a-la-personne-comparatif-europe.pdf. [158]

DGFiP (2021), *Déclarations 2042 nationales revenus*, https://www.impots.gouv.fr/portail/statistiques. [70]

Doerr, A. and S. Necker (forthcoming), "Collaborative Tax Evasion in the Provision of Services to Consumers—A Field Experiment", *American Economic Journal: Economic Policy*, https://www.aeaweb.org/articles?id=10.1257/pol.20190675&&from=f. [11]

EFCI (2020), *The Cleaning Industry in Europe: EFCI's Report 2020*, https://www.efci.eu/wp-content/uploads/flipbooks/2/. [6]

EFSI (2018), *PHS Industry Monitor: Statistical overview of the personal and household services sector in the European Unio*, http://www.efsi-europe.eu/fileadmin/MEDIA/publications/2018/PHS_Industry_monitor_April_2018.pdf. [5]

EFSI (2013), *Public interventions' earn-back effects and the economic rationale of supporting the formal supply of personal and household services*, http://www.efsi-europe.eu/fileadmin/MEDIA/publications/Public_interventions_earn-back_effects_and_the_economic_rationale_of_supporting_the_formal_supply_of_PHS_December_2013.pdf. [139]

EFSI (2013), *White book on personal and household services in ten EU Member States*, http://www.efsi-europe.eu/fileadmin/MEDIA/Event/5th_European_Conference/White_book_final_december_2013.pdf. [144]

Ekonomifakta (2020), *RUT deduction*, https://www.ekonomifakta.se/Fakta/Foretagande/Naringslivet/rut-avdrag/. [128]

Enste, D. (2019), "Haushaltshilfe: Keine Entlastung in Sicht", *IW-Kurzbericht*, Vol. 42, https://www.iwkoeln.de/studien/iw-kurzberichte/beitrag/dominik-h-enste-keine-entlastung- [8]

in-sicht-435331.html.

Enste, D. (2017), *Arbeitsplatz Privathaushalt: Minijobs und Schwarzarbeit von Haushaltshilfen*, https://www.iwkoeln.de/fileadmin/publikationen/2017/361031/Gutachten_IW-Akademie_Arbeitsplatz_Privathaushalt_2017.pdf. [132]

Enste, D. and C. Heldman (2017), *Arbeitsplatz Privathaushalt: Minijobs und Schwarzarbeit von Haushaltshilfen*, https://www.iwkoeln.de/fileadmin/publikationen/2017/361031/Gutachten_IW-Akademie_Arbeitsplatz_Privathaushalt_2017.pdf. [161]

Eurofound (2020), *Industrial relations: Minimum wages in low-paid sectoral collective agreements*, https://euagenda.eu/upload/publications/wpef20017.pdf.pdf. [105]

Eurofound (2018), *Privilege or necessity? The working lives of people with multiple jobs*, Publications Office of the European Union, Luxembourg, https://www.eurofound.europa.eu/sites/default/files/ef_publication/field_ef_document/ef20006en.pdf. [159]

European Commission (2018), *An analysis of Personal and Household Services to support work life balance for working parents and carers: Synthesis Report*, https://ec.europa.eu/social/BlobServlet?docId=20330&langId=en. [7]

European Commission (2018), *Labour Market Policy Thematic Review 2018: An analysis of Personal and Household Services to support work life balance for working parents and carers - Belgium*, https://ec.europa.eu/social/BlobServlet?docId=20319&langId=en. [88]

European Commission (2018), *Labour Market Policy Thematic Review 2018: An analysis of Personal and Household Services to support work life balance for working parents and carers - Denmark*, https://vbn.aau.dk/ws/portalfiles/portal/300252270/PK_Madsen_FINAL_DK_ECE_TR_PHS_May18_final.pdf. [145]

European Commission (2015), *Personal and household services: Finland*, http://ec.europa.eu/social/BlobServlet?docId=14437&langId=en. [103]

European Commission (2015), *Thematic review on personal and household services*, http://ec.europa.eu/social/BlobServlet?docId=14435&langId=en. [12]

Evertsson, M. (2014), "Gender Ideology and the Sharing of Housework and Child Care in Sweden", *Journal of Family Issues*, Vol. 35/7, pp. 927-949, http://dx.doi.org/10.1177/0192513x14522239. [38]

Farré, L. et al. (2020), "How the Covid-19 Lockdown Affected Gender Inequality in Paid and Unpaid Work in Spain", *IZA Discussion Paper*, Vol. 13434. [40]

Feld, L. and F. Schneider (2010), "Survey on the shadow economy and undeclared earnings in OECD countries.", *German Economic Review*, Vol. 11/2, pp. 109-149, https://doi.org/10.1111/j.1468-0475.2010.00509.x. [9]

Forman, J. (2010), "Using Refundable Tax Credits to Help Low-income Taxpayers: What Do We Know and What Can We Learn from Other Countries?", *eJournal of Tax Research*, Vol. 8/2, pp. 128-161. [65]

German Federal Ministry of Family Affairs, Senior Citizens, Women and Youth (2011), *Machbarkeitsstudie „Haushaltsnahe Dienstleistungen für Wiedereinsteigerinnen"*, https://www.bmfsfj.de/bmfsfj/service/publikationen/machbarkeitsstudie-haushaltsnahe-dienstleistungen-fuer-wiedereinsteigerinnen--80542. [163]

Gimenez-Nadal, J. and J. Molina (2020), "The Gender Gap in Time Allocation in Europe", *IZA Discussion Paper*, Vol. 13461, http://www.iza.org (accessed on 21 January 2021). [34]

Gimenez-Nadal, J. and A. Sevilla (2012), "Trends in time allocation: A cross-country analysis", *European Economic Review*, Vol. 56/6, pp. 1338-1359, http://dx.doi.org/10.1016/j.euroecorev.2012.02.011. [32]

Grabka, M., C. Braband and K. Göbler (2020), "Beschäftigte in Minijobs sind VerliererInnen der", *DIW Wochenbericht*, Vol. 45, https://www.diw.de/documents/publikationen/73/diw_01.c.802041.de/20-45-1.pdf. [26]

Guiraudon, V. and C. Ledoux (2015), "The Politics of Tax Exemptions for Household Services in France", in *The Political Economy of Household Services in Europe*, Palgrave Macmillan UK, London, http://dx.doi.org/10.1057/9781137473721_2. [59]

Halldén, K. and A. Stenberg (2018), "The relationship between hours of outsourced domestic services and female earnings: Evidence from a Swedish tax reform", *Research in Social Stratification and Mobility*, Vol. 55, pp. 120-133, http://www.nationalekonomi.se/sites/default/files/2015/03/43-2-khas.pdf. [136]

Hank, K. and A. Steinbach (2020), "The virus changed everything, didn't it? Couples' division of housework and childcare before and during the Corona crisis", *Journal of Family Research*, http://dx.doi.org/10.20377/jfr-488. [49]

Harju, J. et al. (2021), *Does Household Tax Credit Increase Demand and Employment in the Service Sector?*, https://julkaisut.valtioneuvosto.fi/handle/10024/162682. [83]

Heisig, J. (2011), "Who Does More Housework: Rich or Poor?: A Comparison of 33 Countries", *American Sociological Review*, Vol. 76/1, pp. 74-99, https://doi.org/10.1177/0003122410396194. [56]

Hiilamo, H. (2015), "The Politics of Domestic Outsourcing in Finland and Sweden", in *The Political Economy of Household Services in Europe*, Palgrave Macmillan UK, London, http://dx.doi.org/10.1057/9781137473721_4. [85]

Hipp, L. and M. Bünning (2020), "Parenthood as a driver of increased gender inequality during COVID-19? Exploratory evidence from Germany", *European Societies*, Vol. 23/sup1, pp. S658-S673, http://dx.doi.org/10.1080/14616696.2020.1833229. [47]

Holts, K. et al. (2019), *The platformisation of work in Europe*, https://www.feps-europe.eu/resources/publications/686-the-platformisation-of-work-in-europe.html. [19]

Hupkau, C. and B. Petrongolo (2020), "Work, Care and Gender during the COVID-19 Crisis*", *Fiscal Studies*, Vol. 41/3, pp. 623-651, http://dx.doi.org/10.1111/1475-5890.12245. [42]

IDEA Consult (2020), *Evaluation du système des Titres-Services pour les emplois et services de proximité en Région de Bruxelles-Capitale en 2019*, https://economie-emploi.brussels/media/898/download. [95]

IDEA Consult (2019), *De terugverdieneffecten van het dienstenchequestelsel*, https://publicaties.vlaanderen.be/view-file/36716. [140]

IDEA Consult (2018), *Une vision à 360° sur les titres-services*, https://www.ideaconsult.be/images/Finaal_eindrapport_360_zicht_op_dienstencheques-_FR.pdf. [100]

ILO (2021), *Making decent work a reality for domestic workers: Progress and prospects ten years after the adoption*, https://www.ilo.org/wcmsp5/groups/public/---dgreports/---dcomm/---publ/documents/publication/wcms_802551.pdf. [120]

ILO (2018), *Care Work and Care Jobs for the Future of Decent Work*, https://www.ilo.org/wcmsp5/groups/public/---dgreports/---dcomm/---publ/documents/publication/wcms_633135.pdf. [164]

ILO (2012), *International Standard Classifi cation of Occupations: Structure, group defi nitions and correspondence tables*, https://www.ilo.org/public/english/bureau/stat/isco/docs/publication08.pdf. [160]

Istituto Nazionale Previdenza Sociale (2020), *Dati sui nuovi rapporti di lavoro: Gennaio - Dicembre 2019*, https://www.inps.it/docallegatiNP/Mig/Dati_analisi_bilanci/Osservatori_statistici/Osservatorio_precariato/Osservatorio_Precariato_Gen_Dic_2019.pdf. [150]

Jaehrling, K. and C. Weinkopf (2020), *PHS-QUALITY Project: Country Report - Germany*, https://aias-hsi.uva.nl/binaries/content/assets/subsites/hugo-sinzheimer-institute/phs-quality/country-report-germany..pdf. [114]

Jansen, N. and N. Ramos Martin (2020), *PHS QUALITY Project: Country Report - The Netherlands*, https://aias-hsi.uva.nl/binaries/content/assets/subsites/hugo-sinzheimer-institute/phs-quality/country-report-the-netherlandsextended.pdf. [152]

Jokela, M. (2017), "The Role of Domestic Employment Policies in Shaping Precarious Work", *Social Policy & Administration*, Vol. 51/2, pp. 286-307, http://dx.doi.org/10.1111/spol.12288. [58]

Juncke, D., L. Krämer and H. Weinelt (2019), *Förderung haushaltsnaher Dienstleistungen. Implementierung eines Fördermodells für haushaltsnahe Dienstleistungen.*, https://www.hs-fulda.de/fileadmin/user_upload/FB_Oe/PQHD/Prognos_2019_Haushaltsnahe_Dienstleistungen.pdf. [92]

Kagnicioglu, D. (2017), "The Role Of Women In Working Life In Turkey", *Sustainable Development and Planning*, Vol. 9, http://dx.doi.org/10.2495/sdp170301. [37]

Kosonen, T. (2015), "More and cheaper haircuts after VAT cut? On the efficiency and incidence of service sector consumption taxes", *Journal of Public Economics*, Vol. 131, pp. 87-100, http://dx.doi.org/10.1016/j.jpubeco.2015.09.006. [135]

Kostyshyna, O. and C. Luu (2019), "The Size and Characteristics of Informal ("Gig") Work in Canada", *Bank of Canada Staff Analytical Note*, Vol. 6, https://www.bankofcanada.ca/wp-content/uploads/2019/02/san2019-6.pdf. [16]

Kreyenfeld, M. et al. (2020), "Coronavirus & Care: How the Coronavirus Crisis Affected Fathers' Involvement in Germany", *SOEPpapers on Multidisciplinary Panel Data Research*, https://ideas.repec.org/p/diw/diwsop/diw_sp1096.html (accessed on 25 January 2021). [46]

Landefeld, J., B. Fraumeni and C. Vojtech (2009), "ACCOUNTING FOR HOUSEHOLD PRODUCTION: A PROTOTYPE SATELLITE ACCOUNT USING THE AMERICAN TIME USE SURVEY", *Review of Income and Wealth*, Vol. 55/2, pp. 205-225, http://dx.doi.org/10.1111/j.1475-4991.2009.00319.x. [54]

Lane, M. (2020), "Regulating platform work in the digital age". [22]

Lebrun, J. (2021), *La Complexite Des Estimations du Nombre D'Emplois Generes Par Le Travail Domestique en Europe*. [14]

Lebrun, J. and A. Fourna (2016), "La politique de soutien aux services à la personne", *Trésor-Eco*, Vol. 175, https://www.tresor.economie.gouv.fr/Articles/4b8c6de3-e636-40e2-922e-294afb8c74c5/files/ebd29cfd-3f70-406a-bc51-f8cd441330c4. [93]

Ledoux, C. and R. Krupka (2020), *PHS QUALITY Project: Country Report - France*, https://aias-hsi.uva.nl/binaries/content/assets/subsites/hugo-sinzheimer-institute/phs-quality/country-report-france.pdf. [116]

Leduc, E. and I. Tojerow (2020), "Subsidizing Domestic Services as a Tool to Fight Unemployment: Effectiveness and Hidden Costs", *IZA Discussion paper* 13544, http://ftp.iza.org/dp13544.pdf. [110]

Lens, D. et al. (2021), "Can we steer clear of precariousness in domestic service work? Exploring labour market pathways of Belgian Service Voucher workers", *Working Paper*. [107]

Mailand, M. and T. Larsen (2020), *PHS-QUALITY Project: Country Report - Denmark*, https://aias-hsi.uva.nl/binaries/content/assets/subsites/hugo-sinzheimer-institute/phs-quality/country-report-denmark..pdf. [148]

Marbot, C. (2009), "Le recours aux services à domicile et ses déterminants en France: Une analyse au cœur du ménage", *Travail, genre et sociétés*, Vol. 2/22, pp. 31-52, https://www.cairn.info/revue-travail-genre-et-societes-2009-2-page-31.htm. [137]

Marbot, C. and D. Roy (2014), "Évaluation de la transformation de la réduction d'impôt pour l'emploi de salariés à domicile en crédit d'impôt en 2007", *Économie & prévision*, Vol. 1-2/204-205, pp. 53-88, http://dx.doi.org/10.3917/ecop.204.0053. [73]

Martin Ramos, N. and A. Ruiz (2020), *PHS-QUALITY Project: Overview Comparative Report*, https://aias-hsi.uva.nl/binaries/content/assets/subsites/hugo-sinzheimer-institute/phs-quality/comparative-report-phs-final-ramos-munoz-k.-2.pdf. [4]

Marx, I. and D. Vandelannoote (2015), "Matthew Runs Amok: The Belgian Service Voucher Scheme", in *The Political Economy of Household Services in Europe*, Palgrave Macmillan UK, London, http://dx.doi.org/10.1057/9781137473721_9. [62]

Meier-Gräwe, U. (2019), *Fallbezogene Kosten-Nutzen-Analyse zum Modellprojekt „Fachkräftesicherung über die Professionalisierung haushaltsnaher Dienstleistungen (HHDL)"*, https://www.hs-fulda.de/fileadmin/user_upload/FB_Oe/PQHD/FULDA_Expertise_ueberarb._M.-G..pdf. [142]

Michielsen, J. (2018), "Can the Introduction of a Third Party Improve the Quality of Work for Migrant Domestic Workers?", in *Migration and Integration in Flanders*, Leuven University Press, http://dx.doi.org/10.2307/j.ctt22zm9zv.13. [109]

Millar, J. and P. Whiteford (2020), "Timing it right or timing it wrong: How should income-tested benefits deal with changes in circumstances?", *Journal of Poverty and Social justice*, Vol. 28/1, pp. 3-20, https://purehost.bath.ac.uk/ws/portalfiles/portal/201109718/Timing_it_wrong28Oct2019_final.pdf (accessed on 6 May 2021). [75]

Minijob-Zentrale (2020), *Aktuelle Entwicklungen im Bereich der Minijobs 1. Quartalsbericht 2020*, https://www.minijob-zentrale.de/DE/02_fuer_journalisten/02_berichte_trendreporte/quartalsberichte_archiv/2020/1_2020.pdf?__blob=publicationFile&v=1#:~:text=Im%20Vergleich%20zum%20Vorjahr%20ist%20die%20Zahl%20der%20Minijobber%20in,R%C3%BCckgang%20von%201%2. [131]

Ministère de l'Action et des Comptes publics (2021), *Communiqué de Presse - L'avance immédiate des aides aux*, https://minefi.hosting.augure.com/Augure_Minefi/r/ContenuEnLigne/Download?id=EEA5B9C3-29A3-45C9-8459-61C8B4DC00A3&filename=886%20-%20Olivier%20DUSSOPT%20a%20pr%C3%A9sid%C3%A9%20le%20second%20comit%C3%A9%20des%20partenaires%20relatif%20%C3%A0%20l%E2%80%99a. [79]

Ministerio de Trabajo y Economía Social (2021), *Seguridad Social de los empleados de hogar*, https://www.mites.gob.es/es/portada/serviciohogar/nueva-regulacion/segsocial/index.htm. [156]

Miranda, V. (2011), "Cooking and Caring, Building and Repairing: Unpaid Work around the World", *OECD Social, Employment and Migration Working Papers*, Vol. 116, http://dx.doi.org/10.1787/5kghrjm8s142-en. [35]

Mousaid, S. et al. (2017), "The Quality of Work in the Belgian Service Voucher System", *International Journal of Health Services*, Vol. 47/1, pp. 40-60, http://dx.doi.org/10.1177/0020731416677478. [111]

NDWA (2020), *6 months in crisis: The Impact of COVID-19 on Domestic Workers*, https://domesticworkers.org/sites/default/files/6_Months_Crisis_Impact_COVID_19_Domestic_Workers_NDWA_Labs_1030.pdf. [25]

Niilola, K. and M. Valtakari (2006), "Kotitalousvähennys", *Työpoliittinen tutkimus*, Vol. 310, p. 95. [141]

Nyberg, A. (2015), "The Swedish RUT Reduction — Subsidy of Formal Employment or of High-Income Earners' Leisure Time?", in *The Political Economy of Household Services in Europe*, Palgrave Macmillan UK, London, http://dx.doi.org/10.1057/9781137473721_10. [124]

OECD (2021), "The rise of domestic outsourcing and its implications for low-pay occupations", in *OECD Employment Outlook 2021*, OECD Publishing, Paris. [115]

OECD (2021), *Value added by activity* (indicator), https://dx.doi.org/10.1787/a8b2bd2b-en (accessed on 22 January 2021). [57]

OECD (2020), *Gender Data Portal - Time-Use Database*, https://www.oecd.org/gender/data/OECD_1564_TUSUpdatePortal.xlsx. [36]

OECD (2020), *TaxBEN: The OECD tax-benefit simulation model - Methodology, user guide and policy applications*, https://www.oecd.org/social/benefits-and-wages/OECD-TaxBEN-methodology-and-manual.pdf. [55]

OECD (2020), *Taxing Wages*, https://doi.org/10.1787/047072cd-en. [10]

OECD (2019), *Good Practice for Good Jobs in Early Childhood Education and Care*, OECD Publishing, Paris, https://dx.doi.org/10.1787/64562be6-en. [2]

OECD (2019), "Labour market regulation 4.0: Protecting workers in a changing world of work", in *OECD Employment Outlook 2019, OECD Employment Outlook*, OECD, http://dx.doi.org/10.1787/b40da5b7-en. [21]

OECD (2017), *Dare to Share: Germany's Experience Promoting Equal Partnership in Families*, OECD Publishing, Paris, https://dx.doi.org/10.1787/9789264259157-en. [1]

OECD (2017), *The Pursuit of Gender Equality: An Uphill Battle*, OECD Publishing, Paris, https://dx.doi.org/10.1787/9789264281318-en. [29]

Ollus, N. (2016), "Forced Flexibility and Exploitation: Experiences of Migrant Workers in the Cleaning Industry", *Nordic Journal of Working Life Studies*, Vol. 6/1, p. 25, http://dx.doi.org/10.19154/njwls.v6i1.4908. [108]

ONSS/RSZ (2020), *Emploi via le système des titres-services*, https://www.onss.be/stats/emploi-via-le-systeme-des-titres-services. [101]

ONSS/RSZ (2016), *Titres-services - Statistiques archivées jusque 2014*, https://www.onss.be/file/cc73d96153bbd5448a56f19d925d05b1379c7f21/ad1f5dd0305b91 b77a7c8d89191d37ae19e29c14/Titres-services%20- %20Statistiques%20archiv%C3%A9es%20jusque%202014%20FR.pdf. [130]

Oreffice, S. and C. Quintana-Domeque (2020), "Gender inequality in COVID-19 times: Evidence from UK Prolific participants.", *IZA Discussion paper*, Vol. 13463, http://ftp.iza.org/dp13463.pdf. [43]

Panteia (2014), *Dienstverlening aan huis: wie betaalt de rekening?*, https://panteia.nl/nieuws/schoon-huis-schoon-geweten-grip-op-de-markt-voor- dienstverlening-aan-huis/. [154]

Pape, K. (2016), "ILO Convention C189—a good start for the protection of domestic workers: An insider's view", *Progress in Development Studies*, Vol. 16/2, pp. 189-202, http://dx.doi.org/10.1177/1464993415623151. [121]

Parlement de Wallonie (2019), *Les entreprises de titres-services (Session: 2019-2020, Année: 2019, N°: 35 (2019-2020))*, https://www.parlement-wallonie.be/pwpages?p=interp- questions- voir&type=28&iddoc=93400#:~:text=The%20amount%20of%20the%20tax%20deduction% 20for%20the%20year%202017%20amounts%20to%2023%2C446%2C913%20euros. [97]

Parlementaire Ondervragingscommissie Kinderopvangtoeslag (2020), *Ongekend onrecht*, Tweede Kamer der Staten-Generaal, 's-Gravenhage, https://www.tweedekamer.nl/sites/default/files/atoms/files/20201217_eindverslag_parlemen taire_ondervragingscommissie_kinderopvangtoeslag.pdf (accessed on 6 May 2021). [76]

Ramos Martin, N. (2020), *PHS-QUALITY Project: Country Report - Belgium*, https://aias- hsi.uva.nl/binaries/content/assets/subsites/hugo-sinzheimer-institute/phs-quality/country- report-belgium-re-6.pdf. [106]

Ramos Martin, N. and A. Ruiz (2020), *PHS-QUALITY Project: Overview Comparative Report*, https://aias-hsi.uva.nl/binaries/content/assets/subsites/hugo-sinzheimer-institute/phs-quality/comparative-report-phs-final-ramos-munoz-k.-2.pdf. [13]

Raz-Yurovich, L. and I. Marx (2018), "What does state-subsidized outsourcing of domestic work do for women's employment? The Belgian service voucher scheme", *Journal of European Social Policy*, Vol. 28/2, pp. 104-115, http://dx.doi.org/10.1177/0958928717709173. [63]

Rickne, J. (2019), "Kvinnor med flyktingbakgrund i rutsubventionerade företag", *SNS Analys*, Vol. 56, https://www.sns.se/artiklar/sns-analys-nr-56-kvinnor-med-flyktingbakgrund-i-rutsubventionerade-foretag/. [64]

Riksrevisionen (2020), *Rutavdraget – konsekvenser av reformen*, https://www.riksrevisionen.se/download/18.185dfea217042689a765851c/1581941851838/RiR%202020_02%20Anpassad.pdf. [91]

Robles, B. and M. McGee (2016), "Exploring online and offline informal work: findings from the Enterprising and Informal Work Activities (EIWA) survey", *Finance and Economics Discussion Series; Divisions of Research & Statistics and Monetary Affairs; Federal Reserve Board, Washington, D.C.*, https://www.federalreserve.gov/econresdata/feds/2016/files/2016089pap.pdf. [17]

Shaman, J. (ed.) (2020), "Work-related COVID-19 transmission in six Asian countries/areas: A follow-up study", *PLOS ONE*, Vol. 15/5, p. e0233588, http://dx.doi.org/10.1371/journal.pone.0233588. [27]

Shire, K. (2015), "State Policies Encouraging the Outsourcing of Personal and Household Labour in Germany: Familialism and Women's Employment in Conservative Welfare States", in *The Political Economy of Household Services in Europe*, Palgrave Macmillan UK, London, http://dx.doi.org/10.1057/9781137473721_5. [61]

SKAT (2021), *Håndværkerfradrag (servicefradrag)*, https://skat.dk/skat.aspx?oid=1023. [146]

Skat (2020), *Flere danskere benytter BoligJobordningen*, https://www.skm.dk/aktuelt/publikationer/aktuelle-skattetal/aktuelle-skattetal-boligjobordning-2019/. [147]

Skatteverket (2021), *Rot- och rutbetalningar, statistik*, https://skatteverket.entryscape.net/catalog/9/datasets/11. [102]

Skatteverket (2020), *Hushållens medvetna köp av svarta tjänster 2005 och 2019*, https://skatteverket.se/download/18.7eada0316ed67d72823f4c/1579510643608/Hush%C3%A5llens%20medvetna%20k%C3%B6p%20av%20svarta%20tj%C3%A4nster%202005%20och%202019%20-%20final.pdf. [127]

Skatteverket (2011), *Om RUT och ROT , Vitt och Svart*. [80]

Statistisches Landesamt Rheinland-Pfalz (2018), *Das lohn- und einkommenspflichtige Einkommen und seine Besteuerung 2014*, https://www.statistik.rlp.de/fileadmin/dokumente/berichte/L/4043/L4043_201400_1j_K.pdf. [125]

Statistiska Centralbyrån (2020), *Skattereduktion för ROT-arbete och hushållsarbete (RUT) 2018 efter beskattningsbar förvärvsinkomst*. [129]

Sullivan, O., F. Billari and E. Altintas (2014), "Fathers' Changing Contributions to Child Care and Domestic Work in Very Low–Fertility Countries", *Journal of Family Issues*, Vol. 35/8, pp. 1048-1065, http://dx.doi.org/10.1177/0192513x14522241. [33]

Tax Policy Center (2020), *Briefing Book*, https://www.taxpolicycenter.org/sites/default/files/briefing-book/tpc_briefing_book_2020.pdf. [74]

Theodore, N., B. Gutelius and L. Burnham (2019), "Workplace Health and Safety Hazards Faced by Informally Employed Domestic Workers in the United States", *Workplace Health & Safety*, Vol. 67/1, pp. 9-17, http://dx.doi.org/10.1177/2165079918785923. [118]

Tillväxtanalys (2019), *Utvärdering av RUT-avdraget –effekter på företagens tillväxt och överlevnad*, https://www.tillvaxtanalys.se/download/18.62dd45451715a00666f207d8/1586366207527/P M_2019_08_1_utv%C3%A4rdering%20av%20rut-avdraget.pdf. [133]

Tran, T. (ed.) (2021), "Gender differences in unpaid care work and psychological distress in the UK Covid-19 lockdown", *PLOS ONE*, Vol. 16/3, p. e0247959, http://dx.doi.org/10.1371/journal.pone.0247959. [44]

van de Ven, P., J. Zwijnenburg and M. De Queljoe (2018), "Including unpaid household activities: An estimate of its impact on macro-economic indicators in the G7 economies and the way forward", *OECD Statistics Working Papers*, No. 2018/4, OECD Publishing, Paris, https://dx.doi.org/10.1787/bc9d30dc-en. [52]

van Gerven, M. (2020), *PHS-QUALITY Project: Country Report - Finland*, https://aias-hsi.uva.nl/binaries/content/assets/subsites/hugo-sinzheimer-institute/phs-quality/country-report-finland..pdf. [112]

Verohallinto (2021), *Deductions by groups of beneficiaries; by income brackets by Tax year, Variable, tulonsaajaryhma, Tuloluokka and Statistic*, http://vero2.stat.fi/PXWeb/pxweb/en/Vero/. [98]

Vlaamse DWSE (2020), *Wat weten we over Dienstencheques anno 2020*, https://www.vlaanderen.be/publicaties/wat-weten-we-over-dienstencheques-anno-2020-covernota. [94]

Walter Eucken Institut and Ernst & Young (2013), *Forschungsvorhaben fe 14/11: „Evaluierung der Wirksamkeit der steuerlichen Förderung für Handwerkerleistungen nach § 35a EStG"*, https://www.eucken.de/wp-content/uploads/Studie_Handwerk_Evaluierung-der-Wirksamkeit-der-steuerlichen-F%C3%B6rderung-f%C3%BCr-Handwerksleistungen.pdf. [162]

Williams, C. (2018), *Elements of a preventative approach towards undeclared work: an evaluation of service vouchers and awareness raising campaigns*, http://ec.europa.eu/social/BlobServlet?docId=19526&langId=da. [68]

Williams, C. and A. Kayaoglu (2020), "COVID-19 and undeclared work: impacts and policy responses in Europe", *The Service Industries Journal*, Vol. 40/13-14, pp. 914-931, http://dx.doi.org/10.1080/02642069.2020.1757073. [28]

Williams, C., J. Windebank and S. Nadin (2012), "Barriers to outsourcing household services to small business", *The Service Industries Journal*, Vol. 32/15, pp. 2365-2377, http://dx.doi.org/10.1080/02642069.2012.677826. [51]

Wolfe, J. et al. (2020), "Domestic workers chartbook", *Economic Policy Institute*, http://dx.doi.org/epi.org/194214. [117]

Zinn, S. (2020), "Familienleben in Corona-Zeiten", *Spotlights der SOEP-CoV Studie*, pp. 1-16, https://www.soep-cov.de/Spotlight_1/. [45]

Notes

[1] The term "non-care household services" might be construed as devaluing the work in the sector. To emphasize that non-care services are as valuable as care services, the ILO in its definition of domestic workers considers they provide both direct care (care for the elderly, persons with disabilities or children) and indirect care (cleaning, housekeeping, gardening), see ILO (2018[164]).

[2] The structure and size of the formal non-care household service sector has been analysed in a range of reports and studies over recent years, predominately focussed on European countries (European Commission, 2018[7]; 2015[12]; Angermann and Eichhorst, 2013[157]; DGCIS, 2011[158]). These analyses rely on economic activity statistics, such as the Statistical Classification of Economic Activities in the European Community (NACE). However, non-care household service provision is not covered as a single activity within these classifications. A common approach is to map the size of the sector by using NACE category 97 ("*Activities of households as employers of domestic personnel*"). This category also includes care-related services, and encompasses only individuals directly employed by households who hold this activity as their main job. This is problematic, especially as female household service workers are the most likely group to hold multiple types of jobs in the European Union and the United Kingdom (Eurofound, 2018[159]). This category also excludes all non-care household service activities carried out by service provider organisations or companies. Alternatively the use of specific categories referring to cleaning services could be considered, such as NACE category 81.21 ("*General cleaning of buildings*"), but then cleaning services outside private households are included too (European Commission, 2015[12]).

[3] Following the ISCO classification, domestic cleaners and helpers "sweep, vacuum, clean, wash and polish, take care of household linen, purchase household supplies, prepare food, serve meals and perform various other domestic duties" (ILO, 2012[160]). This explicitly excludes domestic housekeepers, which are covered in ISCO code *5152*.

[4] In Germany, the *Minijob*-scheme (marginal employment) can exempt those with less than EUR 450 monthly income from income taxation. As a result, many domestic workers are marginal employees (Enste and Heldman, 2017[161]).

[5] The response rate to the EIWA was about 55% in 2015. Even though the survey population itself was designed to be representative, the results are therefore not necessarily so.

[6] In general, it is more complicated to compare time-use levels across countries. The share of time allocated to different activities appears to be a better measure than levels, exemplified by the similarity of the share of time spent in unpaid work across countries.

[7] The Finish tax credit can also be claimed through the tax card, right after service consumption. However, consumers still need to pay the full service price upfront.

[8] Another difference is that the Finish DHSTC is granted for renovation work as well. However, also considering use of the Swedish ROT-reduction that concerns renovation work does not fundamentally change the outcome: the Swedish tax credit seems more effective in reaching low-income households.

[9] Direct domestic employment instead benefits from RUT-deduction on employer contributions, which is a substantially smaller incentive than the tax credit on the work of service providers and generally not very popular (see Box 4.2).

[10] The *mode mandatories* only makes up about 10% of all tripartite work arrangements and has been decreasing over the years (DARES, 2020[71]).

[11] Workers in service provider organisation usually earn more, though this often makes their services too costly for many households.

[12] When services are purchased through provider organisation instead, labour inspectorates can be better able to monitor the workplace, even in the household, and thus ensure better protection for the workers (Ramos Martin and Ruiz, 2020[13]).

[13] The hourly prices in the non-care sector were on average EUR 21 in 2012, while the exact rates vary across provider type and service task.

[14] A notable exception is the provision of a 40 hour work week, in contrast to the 35 hour week specified in the General Labour Code.

[15] Germany ratified the *ILO Convention 189 on Domestic Work,* in 2013. Sweden did so in 2019 and it came into force in April 2020. France is the only country focussed on in this report which did not ratify the convention by 2021.

[16] Among others, these certification tests cover basics of cleaning work, organisation and finances, service quality, as well as health and safety (including ergonomics and chemical product safety).

[17] An evaluation of the tax credit for renovation and artisan services (also under the general German policy framework) showed only small employment effects in the relevant occupations (Walter Eucken Institut and Ernst & Young, 2013[162]).

[18] Earlier estimates for 1995, 2005 and 2011 are based on a DARES survey, indicating a stepwise decrease from 50% to 25%, while estimates for 2015 are based on a CRÉDOC survey. It is thus not entirely clear whether the undeclared household service sector decreased further between 2011 and 2015, or whether this reflects differences in survey methodologies.

[19] The net costs per full-time job vary between the Belgian regions, primarily as tax credits vary between them. As such, the net costs per full-time job were negative in Brussels and Wallonia, while they were positive in the most populous region Flanders.

[20] The implicit subsidies in the social voucher system may go to workers who were already employed in the system (deadweight effect) and may lead to the loss of jobs in sectors that compete with the service cheque sector (displacement effect) or for groups not directly targeted by the subsidy (substitution effect).

[21] Earlier simulations estimated that subsidies in the non-care household service market would lead to earn-back effects that are substantially larger than the cost (German Federal Ministry of Family Affairs, Senior Citizens, Women and Youth, 2011[163]).

Annex A. Other international systems

Austria: Dienstleistungsscheck

Since 2006, the Household Service Cheque (*Dienstleistungsscheck*) is available in Austria, with which Households can pay for personal and household services, such as cleaning, gardening, and childcare. The Household Service Cheque is not subsidised and only applies to workers in marginal employment, who earn at maximum EUR 651.86 (PPP 867) per month in 2021.[1] The cheques can be bought for either EUR 5.10 or EUR 10.20, with value EUR 5 or EUR 10 (PPP 6.55 or 13.10). For each cheque, the 2% difference between the price and the value cover administrative costs of the scheme (Ad-PHS, 2020[143]).

Household service providers under this scheme are covered by some social security, such as accident insurance paid by the employing households, though health and pension insurance are voluntary at a price of EUR 67.18 (PPP 88.00). These insurances are also only provided in the case of regular employment relationships, relevant criteria are met by submitting a cheque for reimbursement at least every two months (Ad-PHS, 2020[143]).

Despite its growing volume over the years, the Household Service Cheque is not particularly popular. In 2007, about 337 000 cheques were used, tantamount to a volume of EUR 10 million (PPP 13 million) (Williams, 2018[68]). As such, the effects on formalisation of household service work in Austria have also been rather limited. While the number of marginal workers in these arrangements increased from 2 038 in 2006 to 10 881 in 2017, only a third of them are in regular work arrangements (Ad-PHS, 2020[143]). According to the EFSI, the system only contributed to the formalisation of approximately 1.55 million work hours until 2013. A primary reason may be that the Household Service Cheque is overall not very attractive to service providers (EFSI, 2013[144]).

Canada (province of Québec): Chèque emploi service

Building on an earlier allowance system, the government of the province of Québec introduced the *Chèque emploi-service* in 1998, after piloting in 1997, in order to formalize the sector and ease access to services for households. The paycheque is available to individuals with loss of autonomy, such as the elderly or individuals with disabilities, and eases the administrative aspects of hiring directly employed domestic workers for care or non-care purposes, in conjunction with financial allowances granted to this group. The *Centre de traitement du chèque emploi-service* handles most of the tasks concerning pay and social contributions. As a result, the share of services provided to households with loss of autonomy by employees under the paycheque is relatively high, making up 43% of all long-term home help services (Boivin, 2017[89]).

However, the conditions for the workers providing household services are relatively precarious. A major reason is that the workers under this scheme, about 10 386 between 2015 and 2016, are categorised as *gardienne* employees, which excludes them from a range of labour protections that other groups of employees are granted. The particularly low salary, about CAD 12.62 (PPP 10.11) on average per hour in 2015, and their variable, unpredictable and fragmented working hours add to the unattractive working conditions on the sector (Boivin, 2017[89]).

Denmark: BoligJobordningen

In 1994, the Danish Government introduced household service subsidies under the Home Service Scheme (*Hjemmeserviceordningen*). The scheme offered a tax subsidy on services, such as cleaning and gardening, costing the Danish Government DKK 600 million (PPP 70 million) at its height. The tax subsidy itself changed at various times, reaching 60% on the service price at maximum. The effects of the scheme on undeclared work have been rather limited, even though the demand for declared services increased (European Commission, 2018[145]).

In the year prior to the abolishment of the Home Service Scheme in 2012, the Danish Government had already introduced the Housing Job Scheme (*BoligJobordningen*). With some similarities to the old system, the Housing Job Scheme offers non-refundable tax deductions on domestic help and renovation work, which are administered with the annual tax returns by the Danish Ministry of Taxation. As of 2021, the available tax credit is 35% for household services (*servicefradrag*), including cleaning, laundry, gardening and childcare, and 25% for renovation work (*håndværkerfradrag*), while a maximum of DKK 25 000 (PPP 3 750) can be deducted for either service per year. In 2019, more than 300 000 persons have made use of household services under the Housing-Job Scheme. Similar to other tax deduction systems in the Nordics, the schemes usage increases substantially with income (European Commission, 2018[145]; SKAT, 2021[146]; 2020[147]).

The only labour supply evaluation of the Housing Job Scheme focusses exclusively on the renovation part of the subsidy and failed to find any significantly positive effects. In terms of undeclared work, it is estimated that only 5% of the services subsidised under the Housing Job Scheme would have otherwise been performed undeclared (European Commission, 2018[145]). Overall, the effects of the scheme must been seen as rather limited, especially as 4 to 10% of Danish households still made use of undeclared cleaning work in 2017 (Mailand and Larsen, 2020[148]).

Italy: Libretto di famiglia

With the *buoni lavoro* system, a first declarative system was introduced in Italy in 2003. The goal of the system was to reduce informal work and to regulate wages for occasional work, such as seasonal employment in the agricultural sector. Resulting from wide-spread use for non-occasional use over the years, the system was replaced by the *libretto famiglia* (Family Booklet) in 2017 (Williams, 2018[68]).

The Family Booklet is a paycheque system, through which private households can pay for occasional domestic service work, such as cleaning, gardening and childcare. The value of each cheque is set at EUR 10 (PPP 15.95) and can be used for one hour of domestic service work. Workers that receive the cheque, who can only perform these tasks occasionally, can exchange each for EUR 8 (EUR 11.97), while the remaining EUR 2 (PPP 2.99) is going toward social insurance and management of the system. Certain ceilings limit the possibility for abuse as in the previous system and underline the occasional nature of the service that shall be provided under the scheme. As such, workers under the Family Booklet system can at maximum receive EUR 5 000 (PPP 7 480) in cheques per year, of which EUR 2 500 (PPP 3 740) can be from the same employer. Workers can also not be registered as self-employed or be employed by a service provider organization. Private households that make use of the paycheque can only do so for a maximum of EUR 5 000 (PPP 7 480) per year (Ad-PHS, 2020[149]).

The family booklet system has resulted in substantially better labour protection and access to social security for household service workers that would otherwise likely to work informally. Workers pay social security, are covered by accident insurance, are guaranteed minimum daily rest periods and maximum weekly working times, and receive a minimum wage corresponding to the voucher value (Williams, 2018[68]).

Despite these provisions and the prevalence of domestic work in Italy, the paycheque is rarely used. In both 2018 and 2019, only slightly more than 2 million hours of service work are financed through the booklet, while approximately 1 100 workers are active in the system each year (Istituto Nazionale Previdenza Sociale, 2020[150]). Instead, most domestic workers are employed in regular directly employment relationships, such that Italy has largest share households directly employing domestic workers in Europe. While declared employment in these settings is regulated by the National Collective Labour Agreement, estimates state that more than half of all domestic workers are providing their services informally and thus forego any social security coverage and labour protection (Ad-PHS, 2020[149]). Overall, the Family Booklet paycheque system has had a rather limited effect on formalizing the household service sector.

Luxembourg: Abattement pour charges extraordinaires

Luxembourg offers a fixed tax deduction for care and non-care households services, provided either by directly employed workers or through intermediary service providers, under the allowance for extraordinary charges (*Abattement pour charges extraordinaires*). Households that make use of such services receive a non-refundable monthly tax deduction of EUR 450 (PPP 531) per month or EUR 5 400 (PPP 6 375) per year. The incurred costs must be declared both to the tax administration in Luxembourg and the *Centre commun de la sécurité sociale* (Joint Social Security Centre). The latter of these declarations generally serves as the contractual basis for the work arrangement. The Joint Social Security Centre further simplifies the administration of direct employment through the centralized issuance of payslips and the determination of social security contributions (Ad-PHS, 2020[151]).

The predominant work arrangement in the household service market is direct bipartite employment and, just as in many other countries, households with higher incomes are the main beneficiaries of the tax deduction. The household service sector, employs about 8.300 directly hired workers, many of which are cross-border commuters from France or Belgium, as well as labour migrants from Eastern Europe. There is no qualification standard, nor regular training, for workers in the non-care part of the sector, in particular those that work in bipartite arrangements. Payment rates for domestic workers is among the highest in Europe, reaching between EUR 3 and EUR 16 (PPP 15.34 and 18.89) for workers in direct employment, including paid leave and paid public holidays (Ad-PHS, 2020[151]).

The Netherlands: Regeling Dienstverlening aan huis

The Dutch Government creates incentives for private employment of care and (non-care) household service workers who are hired for four days or less per week. The Service Provision at Home scheme (*Regeling Dienstverlening aan huis*), which was launched in 2007, exempts such households from all taxes and social security contributions on wages. The services covered range from cleaning and cooking to child- and personal care. In the absence of employer contributions, private households and service workers freely negotiate the wage for the services provided. These negotiations are theoretically limited by the Dutch minimum wage, though not every household employer pays minimum wage to their service workers. It is also the households themselves who are responsible for the monitoring of service quality (Jansen and Ramos Martin, 2020[152]; Ad-PHS, 2020[153]).

The exemption from social security contributions results in weak labour protection and adverse working conditions for household service workers. While regular employees on the Dutch labour market are able to claim sickness benefits for two years at 70% of the previous wages, household service employees under the Service Provision at Home scheme are only granted six weeks. In addition, employees on open-ended contracts under this scheme are exempt from prior consent to dismissal by their employers. The vast majority of Dutch households employing service workers do not pay their workers during vacation or sickness and more than three-quarters do not comply with any of their remaining employer duties (Jansen and Ramos Martin, 2020[152]; Panteia, 2014[154]).

The market for the Service Provision at Home scheme is nevertheless substantial. In 2014, it was estimated to be worth about EUR 1.5 billion (PPP 1.9 billion), most of which concerned cleaning work. There were about 1 million users of the scheme, most of which are generally more affluent than the average Dutch household. With on average EUR 10.5 (PPP 13) in 2014, the wage paid to the service workers is low and a quarter of employees pay below minimum wage (Panteia, 2014[154]). There are nevertheless about 435 000 care and non-care household service workers in the country (Ad-PHS, 2020[153]).

Spain: Sistema Especial para Empleados de Hogar

In Spain, the Special System for Domestic Employees (*Sistema Especial para Empleados de Hogar*) provides households that directly employ non-care household service employees with a partial exemption on their social security contributions. The exemption covers 20% of the regular employer contributions and is increased to 45% for families with 3 children or more. Excluded are those work arrangements with less than 60 hours of monthly work which are bound by an agreement to pay the social contributions themselves (Ad-PHS, 2020[155]; Ministerio de Trabajo y Economía Social, 2021[156]).

In general, the Spanish non-care household service sector is very large and formal employment therein makes up only about 3% of the Spanish workforce (seeFigure 2.1). Direct employment is by far the most common work arrangement, concerning about 626,000 non-care domestic workers directly hired by households. While there is dedicated training and a formal certification system for these employees, it is not compulsory for employment (Ad-PHS, 2020[155]).